*farm*house
*A*LES *Culture and Craftsmanship in the Belgian Tradition*

Phil Markowski

With contributions from
Tomme Arthur and Yvan De Baets

brewers publications

**A Division of the
Association of Brewers
Boulder, Colorado**

Brewers Publications
A division of the Association of Brewers
PO Box 1679, Boulder, CO 80306-1679
www.beertown.org

© 2004 by Phil Markowski

Printed in the United States of America.

10 9 8 7 6 5 4 3 2 1

ISBN: 0-937381-84-5

Library of Congress Cataloging-in-Publication Data

Markowski, Phil.
  Farmhouse ales : culture and craftsmanship in the Belgian tradition / Phil Markowski ; with contributions from Tomme Arthur and Yvan De Baets.
    p. cm.
  Includes bibliographical references and index.
  ISBN 0-937381-84-5
  1. Ale--Flanders--History. I. Title.

  TP578.M34 2004
  641.2'3'094931--dc22

                                        2004023123

Publishing Editor: Ray Daniels
Technical Editor: Randy Mosher
Copy Editor: Jill Redding
Index: Daria Labinsky
Production & Design Management: Stephanie Johnson
Cover and Interior Design: Julie Korowotny
Cover Illustration: Naomi Shea
Photos: Scott Morrison, Dan Shelton and Matt Stinchfield

table of Contents

Acknowledgments

The list of people to thank is a long one. At the top is my wife, Maryann, for her patience and support—before, during, and after this project. More of the same goes to the Sullivan brothers, owners of the Southampton Publick House, who allow me the freedom to endlessly experiment in a commercial brewery. Thanks go to Yvan De Baets, a native Belgian whose passion for his country's brewing tradition is equaled only by his willingness to share and exchange information. To Daniel Shelton, for all his help and for importing the best of these artisanal ales into the United States. To Randy Mosher, for lending more than a helping hand. To my translators, B.R. Royla and Yvan De Baets, and to the Belgian and French brewers who were willing to share information, enthusiasm, and insight into their methods and techniques.

With regard to visual content, this book would not be the same without significant contributions from several people. I would like to thank Scott "The Dude" Morrison for his photos as well as his enthusiasm and superior navigational skills. A substantial collection of photos were contributed by Dan Shelton and Matt Stinchfield to enhance nearly every section of this text. Finally, we have many, many labels of Belgian beers, many of which came from the collection of José Detournay and Stef Caenepeel. Many thanks to them for sharing their treasured collection.

To Patricia Ann Sullivan, loving mother and avid reader. She would have gotten a kick out of knowing that her son went on to become a brewer, and a bigger kick to know he wrote a book on the subject. To my father, Sylvester A. Markowski, who, among the many things he gave me, let me have my first sip of beer at age 5. I didn't like it at the time, but look where it took me.

Foreword

I learned at an early age that beer and hard labor go together. Growing up in the coastal city of San Diego, I never lived on a farm. Still I learned early about labor as my father put me to work in his print shop as soon as I could push a broom. But no matter how tedious, such exertions paled in comparison to the inevitable demands of yard work.

On weekends, we Arthur children were bound into suburban slavery on our corner lot with large front and back yards. The house had previously been owned by a gardener and was landscaped in every conceivable way. While I endured many days of backbreaking labor, my earliest memories of toil had me chasing around an old-school, rear-discharge lawnmower.

Through the years of blood, sweat, and tears in that yard, I remember three constants: a lawn mower that rarely ran well, the sweet smell of freshly mown grass, and a swig of my dad's lager at the end of the day. Even now, my mouth waters at the thought of each sip stolen from his cold, crisp beer. Even then, those tiny bubbles offered momentary emancipation from that most American of labors: the drudgery of the suburban lawn.

Of course I have never worked as a saisonnier in the fields of Wallonia where backbreaking labor was the norm. I reckon I wouldn't have fared all that well. Like most modern kids, most of my days were filled with a different sort of labor. Adults call it schoolwork.

Despite extensive studies, American high schoolers rarely consider the history of Belgium. Although I scored well in geography class, I can't recall being asked to point out Wallonia on a map. Our books and teachers enlightened us only slightly about the World Wars and the role the Belgian people played. Instead of European geography, I learned important things like the capital of South Dakota and the most likely places to mine for coal.

Now, as a brewer with a keen interest in Belgian beers, I am more aware of the country's beer producing regions. I can even find Wallonia on a map. More importantly, I can tell you about the beers made there, even though they are only a minor component of the local economy.

As a brewer, my geographic boundaries broaden with each new beer I sip. Over the last five years, I have been road tripping through Wallonia and northern France one bottle at a time. The rustic producers in this region have become some of my favorite beers including the peppery *saisons* of Brasserie Dupont and the seasonal anomalies of Brasserie Fantome. I also have grown to love the musty cellar qualities of *bières de garde*. Of the beers that I regularly consume, I find these to be rewardingly flavorful while at the same time refreshingly straightforward.

I believe these styles to be among the most versatile of beers, offering a wide range of flavors from one producer to the next. They make deft companions for fish and salads but can also be cellared for many months, held back until they develop their delightful yet understated complexities.

Much has been written about these beers of late and brewers everywhere seek to recreate and explore both traditional and modern farmhouse brews. Students of this realm understand them as the beers of an agrarian society. As such, their character has been shaped less by the fickleness of consumer tastes and more by farm operations and the need to nourish a staff of laborers. Because these beers belong to a "family" of products with, in my opinion, no stylistic absolutes, few sources of authoritative information can be found. This fact hampers both our understanding of these beers and our ability to research them effectively.

This problem faced Phil Markowski head-on when he tackled this project. As brewers, we conduct research on beers and this can be an arduous and difficult task with each frothy pint rearing its head. I know from conversations with Phil just how complicated undertaking a book like this can be. I applaud his fastidious determination and resolve to add to the brewing canon. A resource like this comes along when information is scarce and an author is inspired to put forth effort and a commitment to due diligence.

Yvan De Baets' *saison* essay makes a worthy addition to the text, extending our view of the style. Through his perspective, we can reconsider the *saison* we know and love today with the *saison* of a more rustic time. We may also be persuaded that these beers share primitive roots with the likes of lambic and Berliner Weisse through their microbial predispositions. I love the thought-provoking nature of this chapter and the historical tapestry it provides for the foundations of modern farmhouse brewing.

I used to think that I knew a lot about these beers. But through this text, Phil Markowski showed me that there is yet more to learn. The chapters on *bière de garde* and *saison* will enable brewers and enthusiasts a rare glimpse into the production of these beers without ever having to worry about stepping in piles of merde. Upon opening these pages, you will instantly be transferred to Flanders and asked to pick up an axe to help till the field. As you slog across the mud you'll enjoy the rich smells of Mother Nature at your back, while privately wondering if it's worth the effort. Then they will hand you one of the most fantastic beers you have ever tasted—and it will be worth every drop of blood, sweat, and tears, if not more.

I'm thankful this book has finally been written. It is way overdue. I am confident I am not alone in this assessment. I offer my heartfelt thanks to Phil for completing this book. As an enthusiast, consumer, and producer of these beers, I am indebted to him for his research enabling us all to possess a more lucid understanding of these beers that I know and love.

Tomme Arthur
Head Brewer
Pizza Port Solana Beach, California
July 17, 2004

Overview

Introduction

*T*he term "farmhouse ales" conjures up romantic images of
simple country beers brewed on self-sufficient farms as a
matter of necessity. Although somewhat vague and subjective, the
term generally denotes two basic style groups: Wallonian *saison*
and French *bière de garde*. No doubt, these two style groups today
differ greatly from the farmhouse ales of centuries past. Modern
versions are the result of years of interpretation, refinement, and
reinvention of the simple, rustic ales brewed on farms in the wide
area once known as the Kingdom of Flanders. Today the Flanders
region encompasses the northern half of Belgium. However, the
legacy of the Flemish brewing heritage transcends the borders of
contemporary France, Belgium, and the Netherlands.

For Flemish farmer-brewers, these rustic ales served the
simple needs of personal pleasure and basic survival. The fact
that they were brewed for consumption on the farm and not as
commercial products only adds to their obscurity and makes us
all the more fortunate to have their descendents today.

In the rush to embrace new high-tech lager beers, products of
a budding industrial age, many varieties of farmhouse ale went by

the wayside. Ales with now obscure names like *Peetermann*, *Uytzet*, and *Zottegem* simply faded away. While we may lament what was lost, we should celebrate and appreciate what has been saved. By the dedication of a few small brewers who stubbornly preserved these traditional ales we have the two main branches of this farmhouse family. *Saison* is the more charismatic of the two, outgoing and quick to get your attention. *Bière de garde* is the quiet cousin—it takes time to get to know and appreciate its charms.

While I don't need to state that the Belgians have a strong, deep love of beer and brewing, the French could use a little airtime. The French have a little-known tradition of beer appreciation. While they don't begin to rival the Belgians in the sheer range of flavors and styles, they have a rich beer culture, particularly in the northern regions of Nord, Pas-de-Calais, and Alsace. Not long ago, hundreds of small independent breweries existed across the country. As industrialization drew large numbers of people from rural to urban areas, many small breweries closed. Consolidation squeezed out the smaller brewer, resulting in a few large breweries controlling the national market. The French market was slowly and deliberately ground down into industrialized blandness—and then came a revolution in the late 1970s and early 1980s.

This story should sound familiar to students of American brewing as it closely parallels recent U.S. beer market history. While the French beer renaissance has not had as profound an impact as that of the United States, the French specialty beer scene continues to grow in the subtle, sophisticated way the country has been known to display. There is a greater appreciation of specialty beer in a land celebrated for its many other gastronomic treasures.

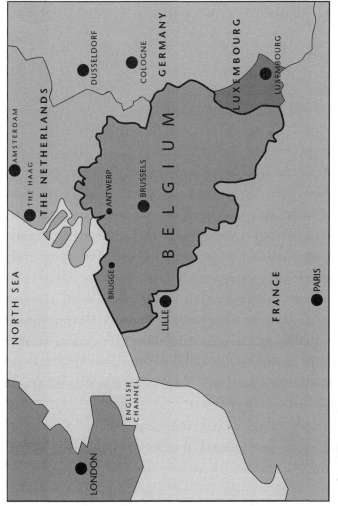

Modern Western Europe
Belgium and Northern France host modern-day farmhouse breweries.

Being an American writing a book on Belgian and French beer styles brings out certain feelings of insecurity. "I'm a foreigner, what gives me the right?" Helping to fuel this insecurity is the reaction from some French and Belgian brewers when I mention that I particularly admire and like to brew their native beer styles—a polite "Oh, that's nice, good for you." California winemakers must have gotten a similar reaction from the French in the early 1970s when they announced that they were intent on making world-class Bordeaux-style wines. Americans probably reacted the same way when they heard that the Japanese and Cubans had taken up the game of baseball. Sometimes the enthusiasm of an outsider carries a passion to explore and understand things that a native might take for granted. Not a wine, a game, nor a beer style is the exclusive domain of its country of origin; in today's small world these things belong to us all.

With that said I deferred to my friend Yvan De Baets to write a guest chapter on the history of *saison*. Yvan is a Brussels native and one of the most knowledgeable and passionate defenders of traditional Belgian ales in the world. His diligence, studious research, and rapport with active and retired brewers of the *saison* style result in what I think is the most comprehensive essay ever written on this enigmatic style.

This book's core objective is to better define two styles of ale that are too often misunderstood. The many interpretations of these styles do not neatly fit into predefined style categories. As a result, many observers brush them off as insignificant or unimportant. But artisans, not industrial giants, brew these beers. Those who revere these farmhouse ales find great appeal in their sometimes wild, often unpredictable nature.

I hope to increase understanding of farmhouse ales by presenting the available historical information and by demonstrating how these old versions have come to be interpreted by their benefactors, namely French and Belgian brewers. Since we can't travel back in time, these modern versions are what we have available to reference, taste, and ultimately, I hope, inspire us to brew our own interpretations.

Two large sections on *saison* and *bière de garde* comprise the majority of this book. In each I include both anecdotal and technical information on how today's French and Belgian brewers approach their craft. I also include specific insights into current commercial versions of *saison* and *bière de garde*, most of which was unselfishly provided by modern brewers. In addition, I provide guidelines for formulating recipes for a variety of farmhouse ales, distilled from nearly two decades of my own attempts to replicate these challenging brews using information gleaned from conversations with brewers of *bière de garde* and *saison*. I could not resist throwing in some philosophical opinions and advice, my own "been there, done that" experience. Through all of this I hope to encourage brewers to think (and brew) in a way that I believe will help them create more authentic farmhouse ales.

Finally, at the end of each section is a chapter with published recipes for producing various farmhouse ales. These are not my commercial recipes for *saison*, *bière de garde*, *bière de Mars*, or *bière de Noel*, nor do I intend for them to be yours. Rather they offer a reference, a foundation for brewers of all scales and sizes. If followed to the letter they will produce credible versions of farmhouse ale, but I feel you will find it more rewarding to take this information and make your own version. Nothing would make me happier than if a fellow brewer read through this text, gathered whatever information was most meaningful to him, and created his own version of farmhouse ale. That is the ultimate goal of this book. Your own explorations will only contribute to the spread of understanding, enjoyment, and interpretation of French *bière de garde* and Belgian *saison*.

BREWING OUTSIDE THE BOX

In order to brew authentic farmhouse ale, it may become necessary to depart from some deeply ingrained practices. Our earliest brewing experiences mold our brewing approach. We cautiously learn the basics, and when we see that those techniques work, we tend to be cautious, dogmatic, and even superstitious about straying from them. This can lead to an attitude that one approach is right and others are wrong. If we don't make the effort to experiment with a variety of brewing methods, we can get boxed in by habit and inflexibility.

To accurately reproduce farmhouse styles requires an expanded view of making beer, or "brewing outside the box." Brewing is both a science and an art, and in any art form there are an infinite number of ways to perform a given task. French and Belgian farmhouse brewing evolved as a "third way" apart from German and English brewing, the sources of so much of our brewing philosophy. Being a successful brewer of farmhouse ales requires us to look at our brewing methods in a new light and adapt our practices to best suit the beer. It will be a worthwhile endeavor.

British brewing has shaped the outlook of many small-scale American brewers—a fact evidenced by the widespread preference for the British "specific gravity" scale (while the rest of the brewing world prefers the Plato scale). In the early days of homebrewing in North America information was scarce; most of it came from British homebrewing books. The common language and the fact that homebrewing was a well-established hobby in the UK makes this connection perfectly natural.

But those beholden to this British connection may find uneasy departures when brewing farmhouse ales. British-style ales are quick and straightforward to brew. By contrast, farmhouse ales (particularly *saison*) may challenge one's notions of fermentation temperature limits, typically well above the 68 to 70° F that many observe. Furthermore, the time required to process a brew from start to finish can be considerably longer with farmhouse ales.

German lager brewing philosophy dominates the industrial brewing establishment in North America and much of the world. The German emphasis on the scientific aspects of brewing is key to producing consistent quality beer. The Reinheitsgebot purity law, albeit limiting, helps foster an invaluable mindset of honesty and integrity in the brewing craft. Brewers devoted to German techniques may experience culture shock in switching to Belgian-style brewing. The use of adjuncts such as sucrose, corn, or honey common to Belgian and French brewing is a violation of Reinheitsgebot doctrine. Additionally, those who strive to maintain the single strain purity of their pitching yeast may have difficulty accepting the use of multi-strain yeast or bacteria cultures traditional for some farmhouse styles.

Brewing authentic farmhouse ales requires an open mind and a bit of daring to push aside ingrained brewing habits. Trust me, the results will be worth the worry.

This book is the result of nearly twenty years of enthusiasm for farmhouse ales, beginning with my first taste of *saison* on my maiden trip to Belgium in 1986 followed shortly thereafter by an attempt to produce my own authentic version. Then I discovered *bière de garde* in its varied interpretations and began brewing my own take on that style. In writing this book, I am honored by the opportunity to pass along things I have learned from years of research, travel, imagination, and plenty of old-fashioned trial-and-error. The information in this book is the culmination of many interviews, brewery visits, and repeated attempts to replicate these distinctive brews. I hope and believe that I have made a few steps toward the noble goal of helping others to better understand today's farmhouse ales and to keep these styles alive and well.

one

Farmhouse Brewing
Then and Now

The rich flatlands of Flanders were once an idyllic setting for the small, independent farms that dotted the
landscape. Naturally, beer was brewed on these farms as it
was an important part of Flemish culture and a necessary
food product. The brewing season at farmhouse breweries
was short due to the demands of sowing and harvesting
crops. For farmhouse brewers, the cold winter months were
spent building a stock of "provision beer" to drink during the
rest of the year. Since the brewing season was shorter than
usual these ales needed to remain relatively stable in flavor
during long-term storage.

Observant brewers had learned that there were two primary
ways to formulate a brew to help keep it stable over months of
storage—increase the hopping rate or elevate the alcohol content.
Increasing the hopping rate resulted in a more refreshing brew,
while a beer with higher residual malt sugar provided greater
sustenance. The two different methods resulted in distinct beer
styles: one hoppy and refreshing, the other a full-bodied source
of energy. In Flanders, these ales would be the forebears of

French *bière de garde* and Belgian *saison*. Each approach appears to have played a part in distinctly differentiating (at least in modern times) the brewing styles of northern France and southwestern Belgium.

HISTORIC FARMHOUSE BREWING

Few documents exist that describe the types of ale made on the farm breweries of Flanders. Their rural origin and peasant nature apparently precluded them from serious scholarly interest. A few intrepid brewing scientists, notably Englishman George Maw Johnson, sought to define the methods of the farmhouse breweries of Belgium and France versus the British (and German) brewing methods of that time. In an 1895 article entitled "Brewing in Belgium and Belgian Beers," Johnson reported on a number of ales of varying strength, most commonly in the range of 6 to 10 °Plato (1.024 to 1.040

Well used brewing equipment is commonly found in farmhouse breweries.

SG). At that time, Belgian brewers favored ales of low attenuation, in the range of 60 to 70%, in order to enhance flavor and drinkability; a thin-tasting beer was undesirable. These low-alcohol brews sometimes exhibited local peculiarities such as the use of various cereal grains, including both malted and unmalted barley (varying amounts of raw wheat, oats, or corn were sometimes added); period of storage; and blending of old and new beers.

Johnson noted that Belgian brewers used a composite of yeasts that "act perfectly" together and in terms of fermenting lower-gravity worts, outperformed the pure cultures used by British brewers. It is curious to note that these higher fermentation temperatures, multi-strain yeast cultures, and occasional use of non-traditional cereal grains are attributes that distinguish modern Belgian farmhouse ales (*saisons*) from more conventional Belgian ales.

In 1905, English brewer R.E. Evans published "The Beers and Brewing Systems of Northern France," reporting that of the 2,300 breweries in France, approximately 1,800 were located in the departments of Nord and Pas-de-Calais, formerly a large section of what was Flanders. The majority of these breweries were small, producing no more than 3,000 U.S. barrels per year.

Production in these small French breweries was centered on simple pale brews in the range of 9 to 13.5 °P (1.036 to 1.054 SG), known as *bière du pays* (country beers) or, in more urban areas, as *public house* or *cabaret* beers. These were ordinary ales brewed largely from local Champagne barley malts but often blended with barley grown in the African colonies. Small proportions of adjunct, generally less than 10 to 15% of the total extract, were often used, with cane sugar or glucose syrup most common.

In some breweries, corn or rice flour was added to the mash tun. As noted by Johnson, Evans reported that extraordinarily long wort boils were commonplace—as long as nine to twelve hours. Evans remarked that the color of these brews was not nearly as dark as he would have expected and that the brewers sought "the maximum palate fullness and sweetness" to compensate for the low original gravities. Hops from the north of France and from Poperinge in Belgium were commonly used for bitterness while the finer varieties from Alsace, if used at all, were reserved for the last half-hour of the boil. Fermentation was carried out at a range of 64 to 72° F (18 to 22° C) using top fermenting yeasts. Typically, fermentation was completed forty-eight to seventy-two hours after pitching, then fined (generally with isinglass) and ready for serving five to six days after brewing. Some of the techniques mentioned define the modern French approach to specialty brewing, notably an emphasis on palate fullness and sweetness, use of a small portion of adjunct (often sugar), and a conventional ale fermentation (when ale yeast is used) in the range of 64 to 72° F (18 to 22° C).

Romantics may like to imagine the glory days of farmhouse brewing as a time when independent brewer-farmers produced wonderful, rustic ales for their own consumption. In reality, these homemade ales were extremely varied in taste and quality. As the name suggests, "farmhouse ales" were literally that, limited to the farms where they were brewed and not sold to a local market. Ironically, it was only when industrialization brought about larger breweries (with mechanized bottling lines) that transportation and distribution networks emerged and regional brands were established. As a result, some farmhouse styles eventually gained a larger audience, helping to insure their survival.

MODERN FARMHOUSE BREWING

Today a national border separates the region of Wallonia in Belgium and the French departments of Nord and Pas-de-Calais, the area once collectively known as Flanders. Flanders was an agricultural region with a strong beer culture and a rich tradition of brewing. Over the past centuries Flanders has been subjected to foreign invasion and domination, shifting linguistic borders, industrialization, and two World Wars. While some farming tradition lives on today, the region has been largely transformed into a modern industrial complex typical of western Europe. On a cultural level, generations of separation have created two distinct national identities with a

This steam-fired turbine engine is still in use at Brasserie Vapeur.

common history of brewing beer. The modern regions of Wallonia, Nord, and Pas-de-Calais may share a love of beer and brewing, but their approaches to their craft have seen the effects of the border that has officially divided them since 1831.

The two most identifiable styles that emerged (and survived) from small independent farm breweries are *saison* and *bière de garde.* Both were formulated to be stored over a period

While most farmhouse breweries now use plenty of modern techniques, sections of the brewery can still have a very rustic look.

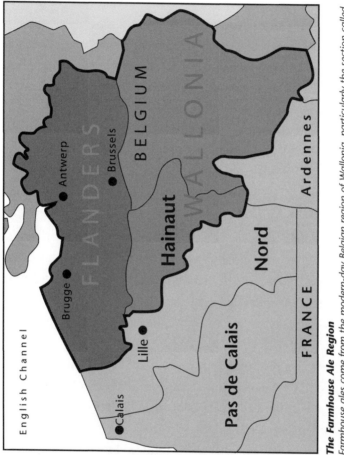

The Farmhouse Ale Region

Farmhouse ales come from the modern-day Belgian region of Wallonia, particularly the section called Hainaut, and the French departments (counties) of Nord and Pas de Calais. This map depicts the modern Flanders region, but at an earlier time Flanders included parts of the Netherlands and France.

of several months as provisions during the time of year when brewing was not possible due to warm weather and other demands. It is possible that at some point a uniform style of ale was brewed throughout the Flanders region; there is no evidence to support or dispute this claim. After the region became divided it is evident that the French side evolved to favor the malt-accented, higher alcohol *bière de garde* style and that the Belgian side tended toward the drier, hoppy, lower alcohol brews categorized as *saison*.

In the late 1800s and early 1900s the region became increasingly industrialized and emphasis shifted from agriculture to mining the vast coal, stone, and ore deposits in the area. This development led to population growth and an increased demand for beer and breweries, particularly on the French side. Wallonia had a mining industry but remained primarily agricultural. There, the small farm brewery is a visible part of the landscape; today, only a handful remains in what was once Flanders. Fewer still have tried to adhere to the traditional methods and styles produced in a bygone era, providing a window into the past.

Ironically, the largest number of surviving farmhouse breweries are not located in France or Belgium but in Franconia, in northern Bavaria. Today, scores of small farm breweries are alive in Franconia as compared to a dozen or so between France and Belgium. The original ale styles produced by Franconian breweries have long been lost to more modern tastes. These German farmhouse breweries now produce the standard lager beers popular in Bavaria as a result of changing consumer preferences. While this same phenomenon applies to farmhouse breweries in Belgium and France, a few stuck to the traditional ales. Fortunately, they were preserved and would later enjoy a renaissance of sorts as a younger generation rediscovered these obscure, old-fashioned ales.

As the Flanders region became more industrialized and transportation improved, larger breweries made the small local brewery practically unnecessary. As consumer tastes changed and old-fashioned ale styles fell out of favor at the expense of high-tech lagers (known at the time as *bière de luxe* in France), many small breweries fell by the wayside, unable to compete in either price or quality with the larger operations. A few small breweries hung in there, producing low-alcohol "table beers" and lagers for local distribution. Others stubbornly continued to market the old-time specialty brews to a dwindling audience. Many of the farmhouse breweries that survived probably were able to do so as a result of low operating costs (their equipment was paid for long ago), farmhouse ingenuity, and resourcefulness that kept old equipment running. A small brewery with debt was unable to compete with large, efficient industrial brewers. Then, in the late 1970s, the unlikely occurred—old style specialty beers came back into fashion. More astute small brewers shifted gears and a market for esoteric specialty brews began to grow, not only in Europe but in North America as well.

While it is less romantic that some of these farmhouse ales actually come from large industrial breweries, it is this reality that has made the styles better known and popular. Acceptance and widespread distribution of farmhouse-style ales paved the way for smaller brewers to make their own interpretations. There are still a few who make beer in original farm breweries; fewer still actually brew beer on working farms. Brasserie Dupont and

Brasserie La Choulette are examples of this dying breed. Modern farmhouse ales have a strong link to their past but have rolled with the changing times to stave off extinction.

It is reasonable to speculate that the glory days of farmhouse ales may be now or in the near future. Today there are more versions of both *bière de garde* and *saison* than ten or twenty years ago, not only in their native regions but also in the "new world" of the United States and beyond. They will continue to evolve, expanding the style definitions to accommodate an increasing range of possibilities. As evidence of this, in 2003 the Great American Beer Festival added a separate category for *saison* due to increasing production of this style in the United

Brasserie Dupont is a quintessential farm brewery that successfully combines traditional and modern brewing philosophies.

States. The number of commercial brands of *bière de garde* produced in France has never been greater than it is today. The name recognition of *bière de garde* has prompted many brewers to throw their hat into the ring and market a version of the style, sometimes with little regard to stylistic accuracy (as Americans see it). With this growing popularity and number of interpretations, these two major styles are alive and well, and we should relish the variations as they make the ales all the more intriguing. As the French are fond of saying, "Vive la différence!"

SOURCES

Evans, R.E. "The Beers and Brewing Systems of Northern France." Birmingham, England: Institute of Technical Brewing, Midland Counties Section, 1905 (223–238).

Jackson, Michael. *New World Guide to Beer*. Philadelphia: Running Press, 1988.

Johnson, George M. "Belgian Mashing Systems Suitable for Light Beers." *Journal of the Federated Institutes of Brewing*, London, 1895 (451–469).

Johnson, George M. "Brewing in Belgium and Belgian Beers." *Journal of the Federated Institutes of Brewing*, London, 1916 (237–247).

Webber, Andrew. "Beer or Bread: Was Beer the First Great Cereal Food?" online at www.owlnet.rice.edu/~reli205/-andrew_beer/beer.html

Woods, John and Keith Rigley. *The Beers of France*. Wiscombe, England: The Artisan Press, 1998 (1–18).

Woods, John and Keith Rigley. *The Beers of Wallonia*. Wiscombe, England: The Artisan Press, 1996 (1–9).

two

A Word On Style

B eer styles evolve out of many things: culture, technology, taxation, location, and consumer preferences. We knowledgeable beer fans train ourselves to think about the world of beer as a grand collection of styles, and this serves us fairly well. In certain times and places, beers do match their styles in lockstep, and may even be legislated, as in Germany. That said, expecting Belgian and French beers to follow this pattern can lead to disappointment and frustration. Brewers of this region consider themselves artists, first and foremost, and the vast range of beers reflects this approach.

For many seasoned beer tasters, one of the first questions when sampling a brew is, "Is it to style?" While critiquing and deconstructing a beer can be lots of fun, a preoccupation with style definitions can lead to a reflexive habit (when not officially judging beer, that is) of evaluating and assessing whether a brew is worthy simply by whether or not it fits a standard style definition. The same can be said of the frustration a like-minded beer aficionado may feel when tasting something completely unusual. "What do we call this? What style is it?" Without a place to put a particular beer, some individuals can be left feeling unsettled.

Style definitions serve a purpose for brewers and consumers alike. For brewers, labeling a beer with a particular style is a valuable form of communication, helping to identify the product and set up an expectation in the consumer's mind: "What should I expect this beer to taste like?" Many beer aficionados need to satisfy an inner drive to define and categorize. This tendency is strong in America and is reinforced by the culture of organized beer judging and beer rating Web sites. In the world of competitive brewing, style definitions provide a benchmark from which to compare and rank beers. They provide a technical challenge—a target to aim for that, when accomplished, can be a beautiful thing.

At the same time, the incessant need to quantify and categorize can interfere with the simple act of enjoying a good-tasting

Brasserie Bailleux puts both "Saison" and "Bière de Garde" on its labels, a source of confusion to many.

glass of beer. "A nice beer, but not quite to style" is a comment of disappointment I've heard uttered time and time again by "style geeks." When an otherwise good-tasting beer disappoints simply because it "is not to style," this is a shame. At that point, it may be time to rethink "style" in the context of good (to style) versus bad (not to style). Style definitions have their place, but they are not gospel—especially in Belgium and France.

Perhaps no other family of beers can frustrate the style police like farmhouse ales—French *bière de garde* and Wallonian *saison*. It is virtually impossible to squeeze either one into a neat, narrow definition. It is important to understand that many Europeans approach the concept of beer styles—especially in the way that they rank and judge beer—from a different angle than Americans. The latter have adopted a set of physical and sensory parameters as a yardstick from which to measure a particular beer, a move designed to reduce subjectivity. The British famously use a hedonic approach, rating and ranking a brew based on the degree to which the judge *enjoys* the beer. To some, this is frighteningly subjective, even haphazard, but not necessarily incorrect.

The French and Belgians use both of these philosophies. They may acknowledge (under duress) a certain benchmark example of a style, and they do tend to associate a particular beer with a certain region or a specific brewery. But as brewers, their intent seems to be to produce an ale loosely in line with a predecessor's, while putting a spin on it to make it their own. While style geeks insist that beers fall in line, most Belgian and French brewers prefer them to fall just outside the line, provided they taste good and are made by honest methods. As everywhere, there are some Belgian and French brewers who adopt a style name purely for marketing reasons or in an effort to capitalize on someone else's success.

This essay is not meant to be critical of organized beer judging or beer rating. Standard style definitions are a great way to become initiated into the wonderful world of beer appreciation. Many amateur and professional brewers (the author included) have cut their teeth in organized beer competitions. They provide a tremendous educational opportunity, and they are fun. The problem with dogmatic adherence to style definitions is that they can give short shrift to unique beers that are hard to classify. In a category where all the interesting beers are on the edge, this makes the style seem a lot less intriguing than it really is.

Saison and *bière de garde* are often lumped into the same category in beer competitions as if to indicate they are basically the same or are not worthy of their own category. While there can be occasional crossover, the best-known examples of the two styles are quite different from each other. One needs only to compare Brasserie Duyck's *Jenlain Bière de Garde* and Brasserie Dupont's *Saison Vieille Provision* to get a picture of the divergent characteristics of these two styles. They are clearly not the same thing. In the next few chapters we will attempt to better acquaint you with these two types of ales that are among the most misunderstood and least likely to be agreed upon by the experts. *Saison* and *bière de garde*—two styles that at times dazzle, delight, and defy straightforward categorization.

Bière de Garde

three
The World of Bière de Garde

M y first bottle of *bière de garde* was purchased in 1987 at an unlikely location, a Puerto Rican deli in Brooklyn, New York. It was a large, cork-finished bottle with a label that simply read *French Country Ale*, while smaller print made a mysterious reference to *bière de garde*. Therein began a fascination with these rustic, malty ales from a nation so famous for its wines that few people ever stop to notice its beer.

Bière de garde is the most notable French contribution to world-class brewing. Present-day interpretations are broad and varied; the best examples are malt-accented without being cloying. Typical modern *bière de garde* has a deep copper color with just enough hop character to achieve balance, and a higher alcohol content than the average ale or beer, usually in the range of 6 to 8% by volume. Modern *bière de garde* has evolved from a distillation of consumer preferences, marketing efforts, the influence of lager brewing techniques, and individual interpretation of how original French farmhouse ales might have tasted. No one alive today can know for certain what original *bière de garde* was like. What is clear is that it was likely quite different from present-day versions.

The farmhouse heritage of French *bière de garde* is well established however, documented historical information is scarce. Much of what is known about these special ales has been passed on orally from one generation to the next. Brief references to *bière de garde* or "old beer" exist in a few historical accounts. A 1905 paper written by R.E. Evans, a British brewing scientist, entitled "The Beers and Brewing Systems of Northern France" is one such reference. Evans describes *bière de garde* or old beer, a popular drink in Lille and other large towns, as a beer "purposely allowed to become acid and at the same time acquiring a vinous flavor." This beer was "vatted for six months or longer" and "on occasion was blended with new beer" in order to stretch supplies (or to dilute sour, old-tasting beer, presumably). In an 1880 work entitled "L'industrie de la Brasserie," author L. Figuier describes *bière de garde de Lille* as "a highly special pale brew made with malt at a rate of 65 pounds per U.S. barrel (10.3 pounds per 5 gallons), aged in large, wooden barrels for six to eight months before serving." Described as having a "very vinous flavor, it was reportedly highly regarded by the customers. No doubt the beer would pick up an oxidized flavor in the cask and more than likely would have experienced secondary (lactic) fermentation, resulting in a sour character.

The higher alcohol content of today's *bière de garde* is almost certainly in contrast to the old farmhouse versions, as a stronger beer was more a relaxant than a refresher. Logically, one has to imagine that the alcohol content of typical farmhouse ale must have been on the low side (3 to 4% abv) in order to maintain a level of productivity on the farm. Evidence shows that farmhouse brewers made lower gravity ales for immediate consumption during the season, then switched to stronger ales toward the end of the brewing season. These were intended for longer-term storage as provisions for the warm weather months. The higher alcohol content of these "provision beers" would have helped provide stability during months of storage or "garding" (in modern times of refrigeration, garding is more likely to refer to secondary storage in bulk tanks prior to packaging). As refrigeration technology became commonplace in small breweries, the practice of seasonal brewing was made obsolete. The brewing of stronger ales, or *bière de garde*, became unnecessary and these ales largely faded from view; any that remained would have been brewed more out of nostalgia than necessity. As older drinkers who may have favored these stronger, more flavorful ales faded away, so did the richer, darker farmhouse-style ales in favor of the lighter lager beers that were becoming increasingly popular throughout France.

The tradition of drinking low-alcohol brews continued in northern France as evidence shows that many French brewers focused primarily on low-alcohol lager beers during most of the

twentieth century. As the economy of northern France shifted from agriculture to industry, the concept of refreshing workers with low-alcohol brews remained the norm. These low-alcohol brews were called *bière faible* (weak beer), *petite bière* (small beer), or *bière table* (table beers). In the more recent past, managers of small, independent breweries began to realize that they could not compete with large-scale industrial brewers by brewing Pilsener and other "generic" lager styles and thus began searching for niche specialty products to brew and market. *Bière de garde* became the focal point of that effort and was at the center of the French specialty brewing movement beginning in the late 1970s.

Credited with pioneering the style that we know today is Brasserie Duyck's *Jenlain Bière de Garde*, an obscure brand that grew to prominence as a cult beer in the late 1970s among college students in nearby Lille, the cosmopolitan city of the region. Belgian specialty ales had just started to become fashionable in Paris and their popularity spread to other major French cities. It was a matter of time that the French would begin seeking their own specialty ales to drink; apparently, they found *Jenlain*. The success of *Jenlain* was largely unexpected,

perhaps the result of "right place, right time" (and probably due to an underdog status, not unlike the accidental rise of *Rolling Rock* and *Pabst Blue Ribbon* as cult favorites in the United States).

Most present-day producers of *bière de garde* acknowledge *Jenlain* as the archetypal example. *Jenlain* was the first widely available version of *bière de garde* and the first to be packaged in a Champagne-type bottle with a cork finish in the early 1950s. The only other potential challenger to this claim might be Brasserie Theillier, producers of *La Bavaisienne*, an outstanding example of amber *bière de garde*. Brasserie Theillier is a classic farm brewery located in the small town of Bavay, just over the border from Belgium. The brewery has been in the same family since 1900 and claims continuous brewing since 1850 (it appears that while Brasserie Theillier brewed what they called *bière de garde*, it was a low-alcohol [3.5%] version; the present alcohol content of 6.5% did not emerge until after the popularity

of *Jenlain* was well established). Brasserie Duyck, producers of *Jenlain*, claim lineage dating back to 1922. The higher alcohol content of today's *bière de garde* evolved as a result of brewers' efforts to make them more "special" (the French have a legal classification of *bière spéciales* as any brew in excess of 5.5% abv). The higher alcohol content helped further distinguish these darker ales from the everyday blonde lager beers that had swept France and the rest of Europe.

When it comes to the concept of beer styles, French brewers have a less black-and-white approach than do most American brewers and beer aficionados. The French tendency is to associate a beer brand with a region or a trend more than to a predefined set of physical and sensory parameters (in fact the term *bière de garde* is a general French term for "provision beer"). If there is any accepted physical or sensory standard, French brewers may quietly acknowledge it, but will put their own spin on it to make it their own. The following description of *bière de garde* and its history is a typical French brewer's point of view. Alain Dhaussy, owner and brewmaster of Brasserie La Choulette and a French brewing historian, describes the evolution of modern *bière de garde* in this way:

> *The significance of the term "bière de garde" is interesting since everyone has his or her own answer. It is first necessary to clarify that the term can designate the period of secondary fermentation that usually occurs when using bottom-fermenting yeast in a standard manner but also a type of beer made in the North of France since the 1950s. This can lead to confusion.*

Here is what older brewers and beer drinkers who remember the era before 1930 have to say.

In our northern region, beer was the main beverage and was very widespread; many breweries, often farmhouse breweries, made light beers in small quantities. Refrigeration didn't exist and only top fermenting yeasts were used. Moreover beer was fermented in casks, which were then delivered to the client before the fermentation stopped, only several days after being brewed. This fermentation which continued in the client's cellar allowed them to have a carbonated beer for a longer period and to be able to pour the beer into mugs without letting air get in which would quickly spoil the rest of the cask.

As soon as the outside temperature got too high in the summer, the brewer would stop brewing. As the old saying goes, "Whoever wants to, brews in winter; those who can, brew in summer."

The brewer anticipated this period and brewed beers in advance that he would keep in the cellar during the warmest months of the year. In our region, this beer was called beer for preserving or beer for keeping, known as "bière de conserve" or" bière de garde."

This bière de garde had the following characteristics: a little bit stronger since the boiling had been prolonged for several hours, darker colored, and more carbonated because it was completely fermented. And the taste was more pronounced, more marked by the long stay in the cask. Moreover the beer drinkers of the period didn't necessarily enjoy it.

In the 1950s, a brewer in the North (Brasserie Duyck) had the idea to redo a beer of this type and put it in a

Champagne bottle and call it bière de garde. A new style was created. Other smaller brewers followed suit and made beers that were stronger, darker in color, bigger in character, and often fermented at high temperatures for taste but not necessarily with real top fermenting yeast. In fact, as in the past, the small brewer used different yeasts depending on what he could find nearby and on the result that he wished to obtain.

The arrival of ready-to-use dried yeasts made work easier for many of the new small breweries but at the same time limited their possibilities to several kinds of beer. One could then suppose that the use of spices once again gives the brewer the possibility to differentiate himself from others.

Spurred on by the success of *Jenlain Bière de Garde* and greater interest in French specialty beers at home and abroad, other small brewers began producing *bière de garde* and other specialties. Brasserie La Choulette, Brasserie Castelain, and Brasserie St. Sylvestre were a few of the small artisanal brewers instrumental in the revival of French specialty ales in the late 1970s and early 1980s. Each of these breweries had a long history of producing low-alcohol table beers before essentially reinventing themselves as specialty beer producers in the 1980s.

Modern *bière de garde* may have evolved from the tradition of making *bière de Mars*, a seasonal ale with origins similar to

German Oktoberfest Maerzen. Brewed in winter when the temperature was cooler, it was released in spring as *bière de Mars* (March beer). *Bière de Mars* had the reputation of being the best

beer of the season, reserved for special occasions. Today, *bière de garde* is produced in much the same way. Typically, it has a low temperature fermentation to suppress ester formation combined with an extended cold maturation period. It seems apparent that present day *bière de garde* has been influenced by the universal popularity of lager beer. Lager beer production is the norm in France as it is in the rest of the world. A cleaner, less estery profile and an extended cold maturation period define the majority of modern versions of French *bière de garde*. Indeed, most of today's classic versions of *bière de garde* bear a closer relationship, in terms of production method, to present-day German *Alt* and *Kölschbier* than they do the quaint ales once produced on farms to sustain and refresh workers.

In the late nineteenth and early twentieth centuries, France also had an appetite for dark, malty beers in the form of Bock. As one of the old labels shows, in ale-brewing districts such as Nord, these Bocks were top-fermented (and generally low in alcohol content as was preferred at the time). This is another source of ancestry for the modern *bière de garde*.

Some French brewers see the claims of historical ties to old-time *bière de garde* as pure marketing (and this is supported by the fact that the sour *bière de garde* of Lille and environs probably bore little resemblance to the modern dark, malty profile). No doubt claims of heritage and historical significance are appealing to the French consumer. Certainly brewers all over the world have been known to seize a popular beer or style name in an effort to capitalize on its popularity without paying mind to stylistic accuracy. The French are no exception. Whatever the case in northern France, modern French *bière de garde* has evolved to become a distinct style of beer, however deep its connections to the old French farmhouse ales of the past.

BIÈRE DE MARS

Bière de Mars, or "March beer," is said to be an old farmhouse seasonal brew, originally from the Alsace region, that has enjoyed a modest revival since the advent of the French brewing renaissance of the early 1980s. According to legend, this was

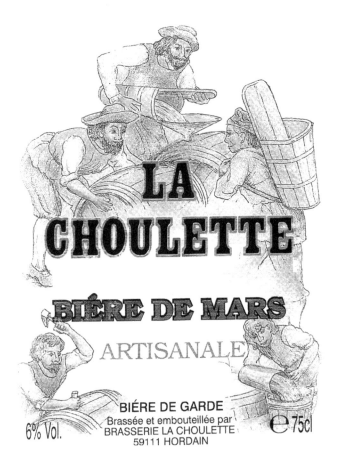

the brew that many farmhouse breweries considered to be their finest of the year. Traditionally made in early winter, when the cellars were coolest, it was brewed with the freshest crop of malt and hops available. It is easy to imagine that the brewer would look forward to making this March beer with the new crop of malt and hops and to ferment it under cooler conditions that experience told him produced the smoothest, best-tasting beer. A *bière de Mars* was brewed sometime between late December and early January and spent two months or more aging in the cask after a slow, cool fermentation. As a result of the cooler temperatures, original *bière de Mars* would have shown a smoother, lager-like character as well as more CO_2 content than the ordinary ales of the day.

Since beer drinking was considered more of a warm weather pursuit, the brewery (probably with a bookkeeper or banker breathing down its neck) needed to generate revenue by renewing interest in drinking beer. The financial needs of the brewery coupled with the French love of things seasonal make it apparent how the marketing of *bière de Mars* got started; *when* it did, exactly, is difficult to say. The claim that it is originally an Alsatian tradition is backed up by the numerous brands of *bière de Mars* produced and marketed by the large industrial breweries of that region (whose versions predictably tend toward blandness). In the specialty segment, Brasserie St. Sylvestre is generally credited with reviving awareness and interest in the style when it introduced *St. Sylvestre Bière de Mars* in 1984 (the name was changed to *Bière Nouvelle* in an effort to expand the selling season). Other small specialty brewers followed suit, producing more inspired versions than did the large breweries. Breweries both large and small have opted to use the name *bière de printemps* (spring beer) in an effort to maintain some individuality while still capitalizing on the seasonal appeal of the product.

As for the physical stylistic parameters of modern *bière de Mars* (or *bière de printemps*), there appear to be no obvious (as is typical of French specialty brewers) common traits to the versions. At least one theme seems to be that the brewer chooses to emphasize either the malt or hop character (usually the hops) of its spring beer as compared to either its *bière de garde* or similar flagship product. Brasserie La Choulette produces a particularly malty *bière de Mars*, by far the sweetest brew in their portfolio, while Brasserie St. Sylvestre emphasizes hop character in its *Bière Nouvelle*. In the modern definition of *bière de Mars* it is typical that a fair amount of wheat malt be used in the grist; Brasserie St. Sylvestre uses 45% wheat in *Bière Nouvelle*.

Today it seems the marketing aspects overshadow the physical traits of many spring beers. Nevertheless, the story and tradition of *bière de Mars* is intriguing and will hopefully provide inspiration for brewers of all sizes to interpret and create their own unique spring beers.

BIÈRE DE NOEL

The brewing of Christmas beer is a tradition throughout western Europe. The British have Christmas ales, the Germans have *weihnachtbier*, and the French have *bière de Noel*. In all these examples the tendency is to brew a more special beer, almost always something darker and stronger than what is normally offered during the rest of the year. Some claim that offering these special brews is the brewery's way of saying thank you to their loyal customers.

French *bière de Noel* is consistent with the tendency of Christmas ales to be darker, more full-bodied, and higher in alcohol content. Some say *bière de Noel* is a long, important tradition while others have recently jumped on the bandwagon to capitalize on the notoriety; it is difficult to say what the facts are and what is simply marketing at work.

In terms of flavor profile, *bière de Noel* has a fuller body and a rather pronounced malt character, usually of the Munich variety but often accented with small amounts of caramelized or crystal malts added to the mash for body and sweetness. Color is often enhanced by highly roasted malt; the palate is generally sweeter and fuller bodied than the typical *bière de garde*.

This concludes our overview of *bière de garde*, setting the stage for more careful consideration of the style's attributes and finally for a close look at how it is brewed.

four

Drinking Bière de Garde

*E*ncouraged by renewed interest in French specialty beers and the name recognition of *bière de garde* among consumers, many breweries both in France and the United States have come to produce their own interpretations, generally amber colored and increasingly in blonde and *brune* versions. The various colors of *bière de garde* have led to confusion among consumers and particularly beer enthusiasts, who tend to pigeonhole beers in well-defined categories. This is evidence that some modern French brewers see *bière de garde* as much as a production method (low ester formation and extended cold aging period) as they do a historical type of specialty beer.

APPEARANCE

The color range of *bière de garde* may vary considerably, from golden to deep amber to brown. *Bières de garde* are generally filtered and most are counter-pressure filled, giving them a bright, clear appearance. Bottle conditioning has become an exception to the rule. Only a few breweries (La Choulette and Brasserie

DeClerck, among others) still bottle condition; however, the majority of *bières de garde* are packaged in cork-finished Champagne bottles.

The generally accepted color for *bière de garde* is light to medium amber in the range of 10 to 15 °SRM (20 to 30 °EBC). The two oldest *bières de garde* on the market, *Jenlain* and *La Bavaisienne*, are both in this color range, as are most others that followed. As the name *bière de garde* became wider known, some specialty brewers began to market blonde and brune versions (a source of confusion to many) in addition to amber. While there is historical evidence of both blonde and brune ales having been produced in the north of France, today's specialty brewer may be attempting to appeal to the modern consumer. Brewers of multiple products realize the benefit of covering the basic beer color spectrum of blonde, amber, and dark to appeal to a broad range of potential customers. Blonde beers are viewed as normal and are therefore most appealing to mainstream beer consumers. Amber beers are seen as different yet approachable to most, and finally dark beers are viewed as special and exotic.

AROMA

Bières de garde express the malt character of a brew over the hops. Often, the toasted character of more highly kilned malts is evident in the aroma of *bière de garde*. French specialty malts such as Munich and aromatic varieties do seem to have more of a drier, cereal-like toasted note than do the equivalent versions made by German or American maltsters. A hard candy aromatic is present in some classic examples (notably *Jenlain* and Theillier's *La Bavaisienne*), which may be the result of

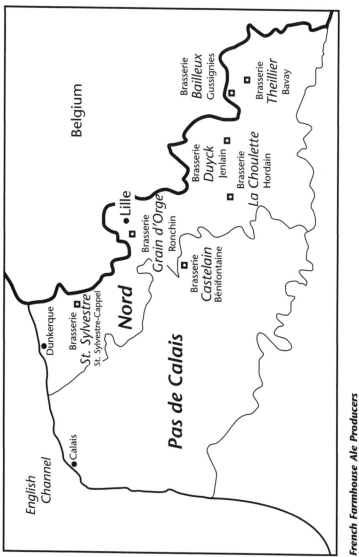

French Farmhouse Ale Producers
The northern French departments (counties) of Nord and Pas de Calais host modern-day producers of bière de garde.

caramelization that occurs in the brew kettle as opposed to specialty malt added to the mash tun. Occasionally, a faint hop aroma comes through in some versions, generally displaying herbal and anise (licorice) notes, typical of the hop varieties used (particularly Alsatian Brewers Gold). One of the more charming and distinctive aspects of classic *bière de garde* is the presence of "cellar character." This can include yeasty notes (not to be confused with fruity esters, generally minimal in *bière de garde*). Even if the beer is not bottle conditioned, most modern examples do spend a fair amount of time (four to six weeks) of *garding* (cold storage) on the lees.

Possibly the most unique note is a distinct "cork" aroma that comes from the almost universal tendency that *bière de garde* bottles are finished with the classic cork and wire cage characteristic of the legendary sparkling wines of the nearby Champagne region. This method of sealing the bottle can also contribute musty and earthy notes that add a decidedly rustic character.

Note: Cork notes, particularly those described as "musty" or "earthy" are contributed to beer (and wine) by a compound called TCA (2,4,6-trichloroanisole) that is present in all natural cork materials. TCA is caused by molds native to the bark of the cork oak tree (Quercus suber) and is present in variable amounts in natural cork material. It is interesting to note that while this character may be considered charming and rustic (by many but not all tasters) in French beer, too much cork character is considered a colossal defect by winemakers. "Corked" wine is considered undrinkable by anyone with a remotely sophisticated palate. "Cork taint," as it is often called, is present in an estimated 3 to 5% of all cork-finished wine and costs the industry millions of dollars per year in lost sales revenue.

FLAVOR

Classic *bière de garde* definitely favors and displays upfront malt character and sweetness, generally balanced with a paradoxical dryness, making the best examples drinkable without being cloying. Some versions are *chaptalized* (sugared) with a small portion (typically 3 to 5% of total extract) of sugar added to the brew kettle. Sugar may add a noticeable flavor, depending on the type used; more importantly it tends to "lean-out" the body and mouthfeel, as is characteristic of the style. The widely acknowledged benchmark standards, *Jenlain Bière de Garde* and Theillier's *La Bavaisienne*, possess a distinct candy apple note, which appears to be the result of caramelization that occurs in the brew kettle as compared with that imparted by specialty malt. Hop flavor is subtle at most and may also manifest itself as a faint herbal or fruity character but often as licorice or anise, flavor traits of French Brewers Gold, a variety commonly used by *bière de garde* breweries.

BODY

The body of a *bière de garde* is often described in the range of medium to lean. Apparent final gravity in commercial versions of *bière de garde* ranges from 2.0 to 3.5 °Plato (1.008 to 1.014 SG), displaying moderately high apparent attenuation rates in the range of 80 to 85%. Of course, factors such as grist composition, mash temperature, use of adjuncts, and yeast performance all contribute to the final degree of attenuation, which is generally higher in *bière de garde* (resulting in lower terminal gravities) than all-malt brews of equivalent original gravity such as German *bock* or *doppelbock* beer.

Review of Classic Bière De Garde Characteristics

- Light to deep amber color in the range of 10 to 15 °SRM (20 to 30 °EBC).

- Malt accented character in both aroma and flavor. Malt character that may be described as spicy or husky is considered particularly authentic.

- Lean to medium-bodied mouthfeel; however, fuller-bodied examples exist. A malty aroma and palate and lean body are considered classic for the style.

- Minimal fermentation aromatics and flavors in the available French versions. Both ale and lager yeast cultures (*Saccharomyces cerevisiae*) are used, employed at a temperature typically in the range of 55 to 65° F (12 to 18° C). With ale cultures this temperature reduces ester formation while in lager yeasts there is a theoretical increase in ale-like fermentation byproducts.

- Long, cold aging period, an approach similar to classic lager brewing techniques or German ale production, notably the *Kölsch* and *Altbier* styles. Generally, cold storage is at least four weeks, but some breweries cold-age as long as six weeks.

- Subdued hop character. In the best examples there is just a hint of hops evident, usually as bitterness to balance malt sweetness and occasionally as an added flavor dimension to the generally malt-dominant sensory profile.

- Musty, earthy "cellar" aromatics and flavors in varying amounts due to the widespread use of cork-finished bottles.

- Higher alcohol content than the typical Pilsener style, in the range of 6 to 8% by volume.

PHYSICAL PARAMETERS OF VERSIONS OF FRENCH BIÈRE DE GARDE

Product	Original Gravity °Plato, (SG)	Apparent Final Gravity °Plato, (SG)	Alcohol by Volume Listed	Apparent Degree of Attenuation
Castelain Ambree	15.3 (1.061)	2.5 (1.010)	6.4	84%
Grain d'Orge - Ambre des Flandres	15.0 (1.060)	2.0 (1.008)	6.4	87%
Jenlain Bière de Garde	15.5 (1.062)	2.5 (1.010)	6.5	84%
La Choulette Ambree	17.0 (1.068)	3.1 (1.012)	7.0	82%
St. Sylvestre Gavroche	18.0 (1.072)	2.4 (1.009)	8.5	87%
Theillier La Bavaisienne	15.5 (1.062)	2.5 (1.010)	6.5	84%

TABLE 1. Original gravity, measured apparent final gravity, alcohol content, and apparent degree of attenuation of several commercially available versions of French *bière de garde*.

ALCOHOL CONTENT

Typically, modern versions of *bière de garde* are in the range of 6 to 8% alcohol by volume. As pointed out previously, there is ample evidence that the alcohol content of the average *bière de garde* has increased in the past couple of decades as a result of brewers wanting to make them "more special" than their farmhouse predecessors. Elevated alcohol content and darker color are indicative of specialty beer status and are the result of French brewers' efforts to distinguish their products from standard pale lagers.

CLASSIC BIÈRE DE GARDE PRODUCERS

Having discussed the generalities of this style, we can now focus on the specifics, looking at individual producers and their

POLITICALLY INCORRECT?

Many brewers, whether amateur or professional, started brewing their own beer to make something unlike the mainstream American brews they grew up with. Some members of the brewing community seem to regard only that which is made with 100% malted grains as "real beer." As a result, some brewers seem to view the use of any adjunct as politically incorrect (an exception might be when sugar is added to significantly increase alcohol content, as in the case of Belgian triple). This anti-adjunct bias has stuck with some small-scale brewers. The fact is that many farmhouse ales use sugar, generally in modest amounts (5 to 10% of total extract), in order to achieve a characteristic dryness and lean body that lends itself to refreshment and drinkability. Traditional *bière de garde* is often made with a portion of adjunct, usually sugar (sucrose) but sometimes with corn grits or flakes. In fact, pure malt (all malt) examples of French *bière de garde* are less common than those that use a small proportion of sugar (generally around 5% of total extract). *Saisons*, particularly stronger interpretations, also benefit from an addition of sugar to boost fermentable extract, commonly in the range of 5 to 10% of total extract.

products. We will start by looking at producers from the homeland of *bière de garde,* the French departments of Nord and Pas-De-Calais. Afterwards we'll take a look at the new world versions that have brought this style to our own shores.

Brasserie Castelain—Bènifontaine, France

Informally known as *Ch'ti* (a slang term for a Northerner) after the three brands it markets as *bière de garde,* this progressive, market-savvy brewery was an early player in the reemergence of French specialty brewing. Today Castelain continues to be a force in the French specialty beer market. The brewery dates back to 1926 when it was known as Bènifontaine, after the town where it is located. Throughout its history the brewery typically produced low-alcohol table beers after it was renamed Brasserie Castelain in 1966, when the family purchased the brewery. Yves Castelain, son of the first Castelain brewer, repositioned the brewery as a specialty producer in the late 1970s in the wake of the success of *Jenlain Bière de Garde*. Castelain shows a Belgian influence in some of its products, which include a triple, a witbier, and an organic ale called *Jade*. However, they are best known for their flagship products: blonde, amber, and brune *bières de garde* marketed in France (and Europe) under the Ch'ti name.

As is the case with many modern French brewers, Castelain employs modern lager brewing techniques in its *bière de garde*. The beers are well made and exhibit more lager-like character than most versions of *bière de garde*. The brewery uses a lager yeast at an elevated temperature (57° F, 14° C) and is said to

BIÈRE du CH'TI ®

BIÈRE de GARDE Brassée à l'Ancienne

"garde" or lager the products for six weeks at 32° F (0° C). Less typically, Castelain is said to use sugars as fermentable extract and the flavor profiles of their *bière de gardes* tend toward sweetness on the palate. Castelain's marketing of blonde, amber, and brune *bière de garde* no doubt creates confusion among aficionados about what a *bière de garde* should be. Perhaps Castelain's approach could be thought of more as a move to capitalize on consumer recognition of the name *"bière de garde"* or as an example that some French brewers see *bière de garde* as more of a production technique than as a historical style of beer.

St. Armand Country Ale
Specifications:

Original Gravity: 13.8 °P (1.055 SG)

Alcohol By Volume: 5.9%

Apparent Degree of Attenuation: 83%

Malts: Pilsener, Munich, Caramel, and Aromatic

Hops: Magnum, Strisselspalt, and Saaz

Yeast: Lager

Primary Fermentation Temperature: 57° F (14° C)

Garding (Storage) Period: 6 weeks at 32° F (0° C)

Other Characteristics: Chaptalized with sugar, filtered, and flash pasteurized.

Tasting Notes: Notes of malt and wood, with some cork, vanilla, and licorice. A touch sugary in the finish. Hop character is distant, but detectable.

Brasserie Duyck—Jenlain, France
Brasserie Duyck dates back to 1922 and is the brewery credited with both keeping alive and popularizing the *bière de*

garde style with its flagship product *Jenlain Bière de Garde.* One of the first *bières de garde* to be bottled (c.1945) and therefore one of the first to be widely available, it helped to set the standard for the style and continues to be the most widely known example. Duyck's pioneering use of cork-finished Champagne bottles set another trend for French specialty brewers, as these bottles are now the standard package for all but a few. Renamed *Jenlain Bière de Garde* in 1968, the product existed as a little-known specialty until, by chance, it became a cult favorite with the student population of nearby Lille, the cosmopolitan capital of northern France. The popularity of *Jenlain Bière de Garde* catapulted the brewery from a small farmhouse operation to a relatively large regional brewery (producing 65,000 barrels in 2002, 65% of which was *Jenlain Bière de Garde*). *Jenlain* inspired other small specialty brewers

Brasserie Duyck, brewers of Jenlain Bière de Garde, *proudly display the family crest outside the brewery entrance.*

to interpret and market their own versions of the *bière de garde* style. The growth and notoriety of *Jenlain Bière de Garde* is said to be the beginning of the revival of French specialty brewing that began in the early 1980s.

Jenlain Bière de Garde
Specifications:

Original Gravity: 17.0 °P (1.068 SG)

Alcohol By Volume: 6.5%

Apparent Degree of Attenuation: 85%

Malts: Two-row Pilsener barley, six-row winter barley, "color" malt, and glucose syrup

Hops: Alsatian Magnum, Brewers Gold, and Strisselspalt

Yeast: Two proprietary strains of ale yeast

Primary Fermentation Temperature: 64° F (18° C)

Garding (Storage) Period: 4 to 6 weeks at 32° F (0° C)

Other Characteristics: Filtered and unpasteurized.

Tasting Notes: Earthy, musty cork notes. Licorice, spicy malt, and a faint white sugar note are evident in the aroma. Flavor finishes sugary sweet yet with enough dryness and hop bitterness to balance. Considered by many to be the historical benchmark example of the style.

Brasserie Grain d'Orge—Ronchin, France

Formerly known as Brasserie Jeanne d'Arc, the brewery was founded in 1898. Renamed Brasserie Grain d'Orge in 2002 after its flagship product (an 8% abv strong blonde ale that the brewery refers to as a *bière de terroir*), the brewery has a long history as a producer of specialty ales, originally top-fermenting, low-alcohol Bock beers popular in France throughout the twentieth century.

Today, they produce a range of unusual ales, including the 15% abv *Belzebuth* and a classic amber *bière de garde* called *Ambre des Flandres*. Located in Ronchin, a suburb of Lille, Grain d'Orge was the only local brewery to reopen after World War II and thus was able to grow considerably in size in the decades following the war. Today their total production is nearly 100,000 barrels.

Ambre des Flandres
Specifications:

Original Gravity: 15.0 °P (1.060 SG)

Alcohol By Volume: 6.4%

Apparent Degree of Attenuation: 87%

Malts: Pale malt, amber, and color malts, corn
   (29% by extract)

Hops: Alsatian Brewers Gold for bittering, Strisselspalt,
   and German Hallertauer for aromatics

Yeast: Proprietary strain of ale yeast

Primary Fermentation Temperature: 72° F (22° C)

Garding (Storage) Period: 4 weeks at 34° F (1° C)

Other Characteristics: Filtered, counter-pressure filled,
   and finished with the classic cork and wire cage.

Tasting Notes: Faint malt aromatic with a nice, subtle spicy/herbal hop aromatic with typical licorice notes. The flavor is malty, yet dry; body is quite lean, more so than other examples (high adjunct portion), well-balanced, and very drinkable; a nice, dry example.

Brasserie La Choulette—Hordain, France
Brasserie La Choulette, formerly known as Brasserie Bourgeois-Lecerf, was founded in the late 1970s by Alain Dhaussy, an early

player in the French specialty brewing revival. Located in the rural community of Hordain, it is a classic farm brewery dating back to the 1880s. La Choulette brews a wide range of specialty products including blonde and amber *bières de garde*. The brewery is unusual in that all its products are bottle-conditioned, a technique no longer practiced by the majority of modern French specialty brewers. *La Choulette Ambree*, first brewed in 1981, is the original flagship product of the brewery and is perhaps the best commercially available example of "old school" *bière de garde*. Fermented with a distinctive ale yeast and bottle conditioned, the beer has been known to develop a tartness with age. The products show a charming variability one would expect from a small farmhouse brewery.

La Choulette Ambree
Specifications:

Original Gravity: 18.0 °P (1.072 SG)

Alcohol By Volume: 8%

Apparent Degree of Attenuation: 82%

Malts: Two-row Pilsener barley, six-row winter barley,
and various aromatic and color malts

Hops: Alsatian Brewers Gold and German Hallertauer

Yeast: Proprietary strain of ale yeast

Primary Fermentation Temperature: 64° F (18° C)

Garding (Storage) Period: 4-6 weeks at 0° C

Other Characteristics: All-malt grist, filtered,
and bottle conditioned.

Tasting Notes: Spicy, toasty malt aroma with a distinctive tangy yeast note that dissipates in the glass. More fruitiness and yeast complexity than the typical *bière de garde*. Finishes with a nice balance between the malt and hops; one of the few examples that is bottled *sur lie* (with the yeast). The latter contributes a unique fruitiness not found in other French specialty brews.

Brasserie St. Sylvestre—St. Sylvestre-Cappel, France

Brasserie St. Sylvestre has a long history of low-alcohol table beers that were commonly produced by French brewers during most of the twentieth century. Owned and operated by the Ricour family since the early 1920s, the brewery was a regional producer of low-alcohol, mostly bottom-fermenting beers until repositioning itself as a producer of specialty ales in the mid-1980s. Today, as a leading French specialty brewer, St. Sylvestre makes a range of high quality, distinctive products that managing brothers Serge and Pierre Ricour liken more to Belgian styles than to French tradition. Located a stone's throw from the Belgian border in the commune of St. Sylvestre-Cappel, the brothers have geographic license to claim a Belgian influence in their brewing. Brasserie St. Sylvestre breaks the typical French mold by adopting higher alcohol content and more estery flavor profiles (from higher fermentation temperatures and the liberal use of brewing sugars) that are more the norm in Belgium. Their best-known product is *Trois Monts*, an 8.5% abv strong blonde ale that many aficionados regard as a classic example of French *bière de garde*, despite the lack of any such reference on the label (there is no reference to *bière de garde* on any of the brewery's labels). Perhaps their most influential product is the seasonal *Bière de Mars* (renamed *Bière Nouvelle* in 1995 in order to expand its marketability) first brewed in 1985. St. Sylvestre's *Bière de Mars* is credited in reviving interest in this once popular specialty brew of French Flanders and therefore inspiring other brewers to brew and market March beers (also known as *bière de printemps* or spring beer—see the section on p. 38 on *bière de Mars*).

If any of their products could be considered examples of classic *bière de garde*, the closest would be *Gavroche*, a malt-accented specialty brew named after the street urchins in Victor Hugo's *Les Miserables*. Gavroche exhibits many characteristics of classic *bière de garde*, such as a rich maltiness and deep amber color, yet displays St. Sylvestre's signature (relative to other French specialty brewers) higher hopping rate and elevated alcohol content. The brewery puts considerable effort into producing distinctive products and dismisses the tradition of *bière de garde* as "pure marketing."

Gavroche
Specifications:

Original Gravity: 17.5 °Plato
Alcohol By Volume: 8.5%
Apparent Degree of Attenuation: 87%
Malts: 80% Munich, 20% Pilsener
Hops: German (nominal 24 IBU)
Yeast: Ale (the brewery uses two different strains for various products)
Primary Fermentation Temperature: 67-69° F (19-20° C)
Garding (Storage) Period: 4-5 weeks at 28° F (-2° C)
Other Characteristics: Chaptalized with a blend of sucrose and brown sugar (total sugar: 20% by extract).
Tasting Notes: A distinct toasty malt aroma and flavor with

licorice notes in the background. A noticeable alcohol presence that finishes with a nutty, toasty malt dryness.

Brasserie Theillier—Bavay, France

A classic farmhouse brewery, this is an unassuming, family-run operation that quietly produces outstanding amber *bière de garde* under the brand name *La Bavaisienne*. Located just over the border from Belgium in the small town of Bavay, this humble brewery produces just over 1,700 barrels. All of their production is bottled and the bulk is sold locally with a small portion exported to the United States. The Theillier family lives in a house attached to the brewery, which dates back to the late 1800s. The original owners, the Lambrets, established the brewery at the present location sometime around 1850. When a Theillier married into the family around 1900, the brewery name was changed to Brasserie Theillier. Patriarch Armand Theillier became de facto brewmaster at age 15 under the guidance of his grandfather Michel when his father was imprisoned during World War II. Armand's son Michel is presently the acting brewmaster while Armand, in semi-retirement, is involved in sales and distribution.

Theillier has a long history of producing low-alcohol table beers, the most popular types of beer brewed and consumed in France. The alcohol strength of contemporary La Bavaisienne appears to have steadily increased since the product was first produced circa 1952 as a low-alcohol brew (3.5%). Brasserie Theillier's brewing philosophy seems typical of many small French breweries—they are apt to brew what the public taste demands. As stronger specialty beers became more popular in the late 1970s and early 1980s (with *Jenlain Bière de Garde* leading the way), Theillier followed. The alcohol content of the flagship La Bavaisienne began to steadily increase over the years, from about 3.3% in the 1950s to the present 6.5% alcohol by volume. Interestingly, the Theilliers do not have any predetermined notion of what a *bière de garde* should be; they simply regard their La Bavaisienne as a typical French specialty beer (Michel weighs in with an opinion that modern *bière de garde* is not what it once was due to sanitary conditions in the brewery). La Bavaisienne is made entirely with French-grown Pilsener malt and Brewers Gold hops from Belgium. Michel Theillier says the deep copper color is obtained during the kettle boil; the brewery does employ an unusually vigorous boil using direct-fired copper kettles.

La Bavaisienne
Specifications:

Original Gravity: 16 °Plato (1.064 SG)

Alcohol By Volume: 7%

Apparent Degree of Attenuation: 85%

Malts: Pilsener malt from Franco-Belges

Hops: Brewers Gold (from Poperinge in Belgium)

Yeast: House ale yeast

Primary Fermentation Temperature: 61° F (16° C) for
    3-4 days then cooled to 50° F (10° C) for 7 days

Garding (Storage) Period: 4 weeks at 36° F (2-3° C)

Other Characteristics: All-malt grist (step infusion mash),
    filtered, and bottled with a conventional crown.

Tasting Notes: Soft, spicy vanilla malt notes with an interesting candy apple aroma. Flavor is slightly sweet but not cloying.

Faint "tea-like" hop flavor; bitterness balances sweetness perfectly. Subtle, spicy licorice character. Very drinkable.

Brasserie Thiriez—Esquelbecq, France

Daniel Thiriez, a former human resources professional for a large supermarket chain, established this small farmhouse brewery in the village of Esquelbecq, south of Dunkerque in the northwest corner of Department du Nord. The brewery is housed in a building that was once home to Brasserie Poidevin, a small brewery that served this farming community (potatoes are the main crop) until 1945 when the owners decided that it was easier to purchase beer from the larger regional brewer (*Coq Hardi*) than to continue brewing their own. Monsieur Thiriez, who began homebrewing in college, was determined to resurrect the tradition of the small village brewery so he enrolled in brewing school (CERIA Brussels) and set up Brasserie Thiriez in the former home of Brasserie Poidevin with state-of-the-art equipment from Italy.

Thiriez is quick to praise his Belgian counterparts for preserving their brewing traditions more forcefully than did the northern French. The brewery makes a number of specialty products with a notable Belgian influence, not surprising since the border is just a few miles away. The flagship product is *Blonde d'Esquelbecq*, its spicy hop character recalling certain versions of Belgian *saison*. Two principal products, *La Rouge Flamande* (named after a breed of dairy cow) and *L'Ambree D'Esquelbecq* bear a strong similarity to traditional *bière de garde* with a slightly higher hopping rate, a nod to the nearby Poperinge hop farming region.

L'Ambrèe D'Esquelbecq

Specifications:

Original Gravity: 14 °Plato (1.056 S.G.)

Alcohol By Volume: 5.8%

Apparent Degree of Attenuation: 80%

Malts: Pilsener malt and Munich malts from Malteries de Chateau

Hops: Brewers Gold and Saaz (from Poperinge in Belgium)

Yeast: House ale yeast

Primary Fermentation Temperature: 71° F (20° C) for 6-7 days

Garding (Storage) Period: Minimum of 2 weeks at 33° F (1° C)

Other Characteristics: All-malt grist; bottle-conditioned.

Tasting Notes:

Spicy character in the flavor that finishes with a curious chocolate note. A noticeable yet restrained hop character adds a unique dimension. Skillfully made and very drinkable.

NEW WORLD BIÈRE DE GARDE PRODUCERS

Inspired by the European classics, a number of American craft brewers have jumped into the production of beers in this style.

Heavyweight Brewing—Ocean, New Jersey

Established in 1999 by ex-computer programmer Tom Baker and wife Peggy, Heavyweight Brewing Company is a small producer dedicated to high-gravity brewing. *Bière d'Art* is a seasonal product from Heavyweight in the French farmhouse style, bottom-fermented and bottle-conditioned in 750 ml bottles. Brewer Tom Baker cites as influences the malty and complex beers of Brasserie Castelain: *Jade, Castelain,* and *St. Armand.* Baker especially likes the deep maltiness and earthy spiciness of the Castelain products.

In creating *Bière d'Art,* Baker uses only French pale malt; the rich amber color is the result of an extended boil of three-and-a-half hours that exploits the caramelization of wort sugars. Cracked black pepper is added to the boil for spice character. The use of a lager yeast strain and cooler fermentation temperatures are intended to downplay esters in favor of a cleaner malt flavor.

Baker says, "bottle-conditioning in the larger bottle encourages the development of the woody and earthy flavors over time, a hallmark of the farmhouse style." The bottle is dressed with a label depicting an abstract painting by Canadian artist Christine Haley. The painting is changed with each vintage. *Bière d'Art* is released in limited supply in the fall.

Bière d'Art
Specifications:

Original Gravity: 19.0 °P
Alcohol By Volume: 7.7%
Malts: 100% French-origin pale malt
Hops: German Hallertauer in two additions
Yeast: German lager strain

Primary Fermentation: 58° F

Conditioning Period: 4 weeks at 38° F

Other Characteristics: Cracked black pepper is added to a three-and-a-half hour boil. Unfiltered and bottle-conditioned with primary yeast.

Tasting Notes: The beer pours deep orange; vigorous carbonation builds a large off-white head with big bubbles. The aroma is layered with sweet malt, spicy yeast, and subtle notes of raisin and fig. The taste is all about a rich caramel sweetness with just enough bitterness and alcohol presence to demand another sip. The finish is accented with mild notes of pepper and hop dryness.

Southampton Publick House—Southampton, New York

Established in 1996 as a craft brewery/restaurant in eastern Long Island wine country, the Southampton Publick House distributes its range of products to select locations in New York City and Long Island. Southampton's offering is brewed for the holiday season as *French Country Christmas Ale*, a portion of which is bottled and refermented in 750 ml Champagne bottles and sold under the name *Southampton Bière de Garde*.

The brew is inspired by several commercial French versions (notably Brasserie Theillier and La Choulette) and is brewed entirely with French-grown barley and Brewers Gold (German grown) and Alsatian Strisselspalt hops. With four to six months of aging the beer begins to acquire flavor complexity from the sedimented yeast.

Bière de Garde (French Country Christmas Ale) Specifications:

Original Gravity: 16.8 °Plato (1.063 SG)

Alcohol by Volume: 6.8%

Apparent Degree of Attenuation: 85%

Malts: Pilsener, Vienna, Munich, Wheat, and Caravienna

Hops: German Brewers Gold (bittering), Alsatian Strisselspalt

Yeast: Lager

Primary Fermentation Temperature: 58° F (16° C)

Garding (Storage) Period: 3 weeks at 35° F (2° C)

Other Characteristics: A portion of sucrose (about 5%)
   is added to the kettle; the bottle is finished with the
   classic cork and wire cage.

Tasting Notes: Doughy, toasted (dry cereal) malt notes with a
tart aromatic from the yeast. Some spicy and earthy "cellar"
notes are evident. Finishes dry and slightly tart against a firm
malt backdrop.

Two Brothers Brewing Company—Warrenville, Illinois

Brothers Jim and Jason Ebel each lived in France, at different
times, on university exchange programs. During their travels,
they were fascinated by the numerous family run breweries
located in small villages in the Brabant region along the
Belgian/French border. Inspired, the Ebel brothers founded
Two Brothers Brewing Company in 1996 in their native
Illinois. Their grandfather, a retired dairy farmer, supplied
them with old milk tanks that were quickly converted to fermenting vessels.

Domaine DuPage French Country Ale is named after the
county in which the brewery is located. The design of the
beer is based on Jim and Jason's experience abroad. These
local farmhouse breweries created diverse, malty beers that
began to detour the Ebels' Belgian pilgrimages. Upon returning
to the States, the brothers discovered the downside of their
discovery—a complete void of the style in America. Being
careful to avoid a *saison* or *bière de garde* style, the Ebels
worked to keep their interpretation of the Brabant style alive.
Domaine DuPage French Country Ale was first launched in
their home market as a seasonal to test the viability of the
style; it is now Two Brothers' bestselling product.

Domaine DuPage French Country Ale ("Brabant-style Ale")
Specifications:

Original Gravity: 15.9 °Plato (1.064 SG)

Alcohol by Volume: 5.9%

Apparent Degree of Attenuation: 74%

Malts: Pilsener, Vienna, Munich, Caramel Wheat,
   Caramel Munich, and Aromatic

Hops: Northern Brewer and Hallertauer

Yeast: Ale

Primary Fermentation Temperature: 66° F (19° C)

Garding (Storage) Period: 2 weeks at 38° F (3° C)

Tasting Notes: Deep amber color with toasty sweet caramel start, it finishes with just enough hops to clean off the palate. Finishes with a faint sour note as appropriate for the style.

Brewing Bière de Garde

five

Having examined the culture of _bière de garde_ from its humble and obscure history to its modern day flavors and interpretations, we can turn to the task that interests brewers most: the production of the beer itself. We'll begin by looking at current brewing practices among European producers before considering the methods and ingredients that work well for those producing this style in North America.

CURRENT FRENCH BREWING PRACTICES

As we turn our attention to the production of _bière de garde_, we'll do well to start at the source to see what we can learn from those with generations of experience in this art. We'll review French practices with regard to important process variables and also consider each ingredient, beginning with water.

Water

The northern coastal area of France, which includes the departments of Nord and Pas-de-Calais, is largely comprised of chalk (the legendary White Cliffs of Dover are just across the English Channel) or calcium carbonate, which gives a natural alkalinity to the water in this part of the country. Values shown in Table 3 on page 74 are averages taken from water sample analyses provided by two *bière de garde* breweries in the French departments of Nord and Pas-de-Calais.

Brewing water such as that which fits profile shown in the table contains a high amount of temporary (bicarbonate) hardness and will have enough residual alkalinity to raise the pH of the mash if left untreated. With this tendency toward alkalinity in the native water, most brewers in northeast France find it necessary to lower the pH, commonly with additions of food-grade lactic acid.

Malt

The typical malts used in the north of France include two-row barley of the Plaisant, Escourgeon (six-row winter barley), Carambri, Nevada, and Prisma varieties. Much of this barley is grown in the Champagne and Nord regions, considered to have outstanding conditions for producing high quality malt. French brewers are interested in using locally grown barley, not entirely for economic reasons or convenience, but to earn the right to claim an *Appellation Controlee* on the label indicating that the brewer used mostly regional ingredients, which carries considerable weight with French consumers.

Classic examples of French *bière de garde* exhibit a malty sweetness with a toasty, husky character on the palate, even the blonde versions. This huskiness seems to be a characteristic of French barley and may increase as a result of untreated alkalinity in the water.

Other Fermentables

French *bière de garde* is not necessarily designed around an all-malt grist. Small to moderate amounts of adjunct are sometimes added to enhance dryness and lean out the body of the brew (in some cases the reasons are purely economic). Some brewers add a small portion of sugar or glucose syrup, probably in the range of 5 to 10% of the total extract. At least one brewer, Brasserie Grain d'Orge (formerly known as Brasserie Jeanne d'Arc) is a notable exception in that it uses corn grits in the mash of its amber *bière de garde, Ambre des Flandres,* at a rate of 25% by extract.

A few brewers, Brasserie Theillier for example, proudly proclaim that their products are pure malt, suggesting a more special, full-bodied, and "honest" brew. All-malt formulations, however, seem to be the exception to the rule as most *bière de garde* producers use at least a modest proportion of adjunct.

The brewhouse at Brasserie Theillier is located in an old city hay loft.

Mashing

A typical mash temperature program for an all-malt *bière de garde* is intended to maximize production of fermentable sugars. While most modern malts are modified to the point that a protein rest is not required, many brewers still prefer to perform one, partly out of habit or tradition. On a practical level, the saccharification is generally on the lower end of the typical range to encourage high fermentability.

One brewery uses the following mash program intended to maximize production of fermentable sugars.

Mash in at 113° F (45° C) – Hold for 30 minutes
Heat to 131° F (55° C) – Hold for 15 minutes
Heat to 144° F (62° C) – Hold for 30 minutes
Heat to 154° F (68° C) – Hold for 15 minutes
Heat to 165° F (74° C) – Mash Off

Hops

French brewers, as might be expected, use mostly (but not necessarily 100%) French hops in their brewing. Typically, these hops are grown in Alsace, a department that borders the famous German hop growing region of Hallertauer. The most common varieties used are Strisselspalt, Brewers Gold, and Nugget.

The use of German hops is not uncommon with French brewers. Some brewers cite the use of German hops as tradition, a practice that seems to stem from the popularity of Pilsener-style lagers, which were probably originally formulated by German brewing consultants for the French market. Another reason may be the German dominance of the Continental hop market as well as a general decline in the French hop growing industry. Ironically, imported Continental hops are often less expensive than French grown hops.

Hop character is subtle in French *bière de garde*. In the best examples, bitterness is poised just at the threshold of balancing the malt sweetness. It is never obtrusive, gently lingering in the background. Bitterness values provided by French *bière de garde* brewers show a range of 18 to 25 IBU. Typical varieties used for bitterness are Alsatian Brewers Gold (6 to 8% alpha acids) and Nugget (8 to 12% alpha).

Yeast

Most French specialty brewers appear to have a somewhat relaxed approach to yeast strain selection. Some use ale cultures (at reduced temperatures) while others prefer to use lager

Plate and frame filter with rustic farmhouse charm.

strains at elevated temperatures. Generally, the emphasis is on achieving restrained fruitiness and higher-than-typical attenuation from the yeast. There are some brewers who claim to use multiple strains in their breweries (Brasserie Duyck and St. Sylvestre, for example) in order to achieve a subtle complexity. Others (Castelain and Terken's) use only a lager strain at an elevated temperature, in the range of 57 to 60° F (14 to 16° C).

One French *bière de garde* that stresses yeast flavor contribution above others is Brasserie La Choulette, whose distinctive ale yeast exhibits a tart fruitiness, particularly after a few months of aging. This could accurately be called an old-fashioned approach, as the otherwise universal tendency to use a neutral yeast strain (either ale or lager) is a more recent phenomenon, dating back forty to fifty years.

Note: Some small French brewers obtain their yeast from a nearby large brewery (most likely a lager producer) out of convenience or because they lack the lab equipment or knowledge to maintain their own yeast cultures. Another explanation for the use of lager yeasts in brewing bière de garde is that some of the current "revivalist" producers existed for decades as brewers of low-alcohol lager beer and chose to use a yeast strain that they were familiar with and already had at hand.

Aging Or "Garding"

To many French brewers, this step in the brewing process is the essence of what defines *bière de garde*—a long, cold aging period. Most brewers cite a minimum four-week "garde" at a nominal 32° F (0° C), while six to eight weeks is cited by others. In this respect, modern French *bière de garde* seems nearer to German *Alt* and *Kölschbier* in process than they do to English ales or the true farmhouse *bière de gardes* from which they originate. The emphasis on long-term cold aging is likely due to the influence of modern lager brewing techniques. A brewer who has received a formal education in brewing science has been schooled in lager beer production. No doubt many of those lager methods have made their way into even the most traditional ale breweries.

Bière de Garde Specifications

Brewery	Product	Ferm. Temp.	Yeast Type	Garde Period, weeks
Brasserie Castelain	St. Armand (Ch'ti Ambree)	57° F (14° C)	Lager	4 to 6
Brasserie Duyck	Jenlain Bière de Garde	64° F (18° C)	Ale	4 to 6
Brasserie Grain d'Orge	Ambre des Flandres	72° F (22° C)	Ale	4
Brasserie La Choulette	La Choulette Ambree	64° F (18° C)	Ale	4 to 6
Brasserie St. Sylvestre	Gavroche	67-69° F (18-19° C)	Ale	5 to 6
Brasserie Theillier	La Bavaisienne	61-63° F (16-17° C)	Ale	4

Table 2. Fermentation and storage conditions of various commercial French *bière de garde* producers.

PRACTICAL FORMULATION GUIDELINES

The following guidelines are provided as parameters from which to formulate your own classic version of *bière de garde*. Considering the wide color range of today's products labeled *bière de garde*, it is impossible to provide a definitive color specification that includes all examples. Keeping in mind that the older, established versions of *bière de garde* (*Jenlain Bière de*

Garde and *La Bavaisienne* from Brasserie Theillier) fall into the color range of what might be described as "medium amber" in color, we will consider classic *bière de garde* to be of an amber color in the range of 10 to 15 °SRM (20 to 30 °EBC). It is on the classic examples that the following guidelines are derived.

Water

Recall that the typical ground water of northern France is alkaline in nature due to a fairly high degree of temporary (bicarbonate) hardness as shown in Table 3. Brewers worldwide generally find alkalinity undesirable in brewing water and this is the case with *bière de garde* brewers as well. The commercial brewers in northern France who face these highly carbonate waters use food-grade acids to neutralize the alkalinity and arrive at a suitable mash chemistry and pH (in the old days brewers discovered empirically that boiling the water before using it for brewing gave more desirable results—because heating the water results in precipitation of carbonates—than if they did not boil prior to brewing). Unfortunately we have no documentation as to the extent of neutralization they perform, but we can reasonably assume that they try to bring the mash pH into the range of about 5.4 to 5.6.

Typical Water Analysis–Northern France

Origin of Sample	Calcium	Bicarb.	Chloride	Magnesium	Sulfates
Brewery #1	138	380	22	12	31
Brewery #2	136	366	43	12	98

Table 3. Water analysis results from two commercial French *bière de garde* breweries.

In brewing this style, we can seek a reasonable mash pH while avoiding high levels of sulfate or chloride that might accompany large additions of common water salts. Under no circumstances would it make sense to add calcium carbonate (or any other carbonate source) to your brewing water since French brewers go to great lengths to remove its effects before brewing. If left untreated, the alkaline water can leach tannins from the barley husk and result in a grainy astringency in the final beer flavor. Alkalinity can also contribute a soapy, harsh bitterness to the finished beer. There are two practical strategies brewers may use to counteract carbonate content that is already a natural part of the water profile.

Food-grade acid can bring the pH of a mash conducted with carbonate waters into the desired range (5.4 to 5.6 pH); however, calculation of the acid amount needed for adjustment is beyond the scope of this text. A more natural approach is to add a small amount of *sauer* or acidulated malt such as Weyermann's Acidulated Malt to counteract alkaline brewing water. This malt is typically added in the range of 0.5 to 2% of the total grist depending on the level of alkalinity found in the water as well as the amounts of highly kilned malts in the grist bill.

Calcium ion additions to achieve levels between 50 to 150 ppm (mg/l) promote acidification of the mash and have other positive effects such as support of enzyme activity and hop break formation. When brewing this style, it is recommended to use calcium chloride for calcium additions as chloride at levels above 50 ppm enhances mouthfeel and perception of sweetness in the beer—desirable effects when attempting to replicate a classic *bière de garde* flavor profile. When adding minerals, consult the guidelines in Table 4. If you do not know the composition of your brewing water, play it safe and refrain from adding minerals until you can obtain a recent analysis from your local water authority.

In addition to these adjustments, brewers find that dark and roasted malts help to lower mash pH in the range of 0.1 to 0.3 points, depending on the types and quantities of dark malts used and the alkalinity of the brewing water.

Calcium Chloride Addition

Rate of Addition (CaCl)		Mineral Contribution, ppm	
grams/gal.	oz./bbl	Calcium (Ca)	Chloride (Cl)
0.5	0.5	35	64
1	1.1	70	127
1.5	1.6	105	191
2	2.2	140	255

Table 4. Quantity of individual calcium and chloride ions contributed by addition of calcium chloride to brewing water.

Note: If authenticity is desired it is not recommended that the alkalinity of the water be buffered by the addition of calcium sulfate (gypsum) as this may raise sulfate levels in your brewing water beyond what is typically found in northern France. Levels of the sulfate ion above 50 ppm have a tendency to increase perception of hop bitterness and the perceived dryness of the brew, resulting in what might be considered as inappropriate flavors (mineral harshness) in classic French bière de garde.

Malt Composition

In deciding on appropriate grist composition for a classic *bière de garde* there are an infinite number of possible permutations and combinations. We will examine two hypothetical examples; the first will be a large brewery example and the second what a small artisanal brewer might use, a grist that contains small amounts of a variety of specialty malts. Neither approach should be thought as better than the other. In either case, the results are subtly different and will create varying layers of complexity.

Reproducing an authentic *bière de garde* is primarily about proper malt selection. Malt flavor and aroma are the backbone of *bière de garde*. The French, it appears, are fond of sweetness and less enamored of hops in their brewing. No doubt certain French brewers enjoy the challenge of eking out complexity along the plane of malt flavors by skillfully combining ingredients. Such complexity is often achieved using small amounts of specialty malts in addition to a base of Pilsener or pale ale malt. Classic examples of French *bière de garde* exhibit a malty sweetness with a toasty, husky character on the palate, even in the blonde examples. This huskiness seems to be characteristic of French barley and may increase as a result of untreated alkalinity in the water. Naturally, when trying to replicate a classic French *bière de garde* it is highly recommended that you use French malt. If French malt is not available this grainy character may be approximated using domestic or German Pilsener-type malt. A small amount of amber or kiln amber (1 to 3% of the total grist weight) may be added to a base of German, British, or American two-row or six-row malt (which emulates the commonly used six-row Escourgeon winter barley) to contribute a noticeable dry huskiness to the palate.

Large Brewery Example

A large-scale brewery looks to simplify operations by handling the fewest number of specialty malts. Typically, these breweries have silos that store bulk quantities of a base malt, usually of a Pilsener or pale ale variety. Oftentimes the handling of bagged specialty malts is cumbersome, labor intensive, and therefore relatively expensive in a large brewery. Consequently, the grist tends to be simple, relying on a large base of Pilsener or pale ale malt. A small quantity of highly roasted specialty malt contributes color and complexity of flavor as well.

Typical Grain Bill Parameters for Classic Bière de Garde— Large Brewery Example

Pilsener Malt or Pale Ale Malt—up to 100%

Optional "color" malt such as Franco-Belges Kiln Black malt (nominal 500 °L) – added at a rate of 0.5 to 0.75% of total grist (by weight).

This approach is inspired by ease and convenience of grain handling and results in a leaner, less obtrusive malt character. The addition of a small amount of highly roasted malt is intended to provide color with minimal flavor contribution.

Note: This approach to malt grist formulation might be more appropriate if a longer keeping time (six months or more) is desired for a bière de garde. As the beer ages and slowly reacts with oxygen (ingress through the bottle closure) the malt character will intensify and come into its own over a period of six to twelve months. A formulation containing a larger degree of specialty malts (Munich, Aromatic, Biscuit, etc.) may become "too malty" over an equivalent aging period.

Small Brewery Example

In a small artisanal brewery the handling of multiple varieties of specialty malts is not a negative—in fact it is the norm. In this environment the small brewer is likely to produce a more assertive product with an additional complexity of flavor not found in most large-scale breweries.

Typical Grain Bill Parameters for Classic Bière de Garde— Small Brewery Example

Grist quantities are shown as a percentage of total weight of malts used. Ranges shown for specialty malt percentages indicate guidelines for "threshold" to "moderately intense" character in beer aroma and flavor.

You may choose to intensify certain specialty malt intensities if so desired.

- Pilsener Malt or Pale Ale (or Vienna) Malt (1.6 to 4.2 °L)— 75 to 100%
- Munich Malt (10 °L)—10 to 20% (optional)
- Wheat Malt (1.2 to 2 °L)—5 to 10% (optional)
- Special Aromatic Malt (3 to 5 °L)—3 to 6% (optional)
- Caramel Vienna or Caravienna Malt (19 to 23 °L)—2 to 4% (optional)
- Amber or Kiln Amber Malt (15 to 23 °L)—1 to 3% (optional)
- Biscuit Malt (Belgian origin) (19 to 27 °L)—2 to 4% (optional)

Other Factors Affecting Wort Composition

Other factors contribute to the final beer color and flavor besides the grist composition. Most influential is the length of the wort boil and the method of heating the brew kettle. These factors will influence color formation during the wort boil and subtly change the quantity of color malts needed to achieve the final beer color in the range of 10 to 15 °SRM (20 to 30 °EBC) that we have targeted.

Note: One small French brewery, Brasserie Theillier, obtains its rich amber color using only Pilsener malt combined with an unusually intense (direct fired) extended wort boil. A U.S. brewer, Heavyweight Brewing of New Jersey, takes a similar approach, using only Pilsener malt combined with a three-and-a-half hour boil resulting in a deep orange color and a signature flavor complexity that comes with an extended boil.

Non-Malt Adjuncts

If a leaner, drier character is desired, a small addition of sucrose (ordinary table sugar) may be added to the brew kettle. This practice, called chaptalization, is a winemaker's term for boosting fermentable sugar content (and therefore alcohol percentage) and is not uncommon among traditional *bière de garde* brewers. Typical percentages by extract would be in the range of 5 to 10% of the total sugar in solution in the wort.

For example:

If a 16.5 °Plato (1.066 SG) original gravity is targeted and it is determined that the brewer desires a sugar adjunct percentage of 5.0% by extract, the following calculation applies:

16.5 °P x 0.05 = 0.8 °Plato (1.003 SG) of the total sugar in solution by weight, from sucrose. This corresponds to approximately 1.8 pounds white sugar per U.S. barrel (31 gallons) or about 4.5 ounces (by weight) white sugar per 5 gallons of wort.

Mashing

It is suggested that a mash program be used that is intended to maximize fermentable sugar production. If using the single temperature infusion approach, a temperature in the range of 144 to 147° F (62 to 64° C) should result in an apparent attenuation in the range of 75 to 80% when using an all-malt grist comprised of mostly Pilsener or pale ale malt.

With modern, well-modified malts, a protein rest is not considered necessary. Many French *bière de garde* brewers still perform one out of tradition (if not superstition). If a step infusion mash is used, it is safe to say that a traditional protein rest may be omitted and the starting mash temperature will be the chosen saccharification temperature, in the range of 144 to 147° F (62 to 64° C) to yield a highly fermentable wort. Once a negative starch iodine test result is seen, a brewer may elect to set the mash composition by heating to a mash-off temperature of 167° F (75° C).

Hop Usage Considerations

French hops are the preferred choice when available. These varieties are difficult to obtain in North America; however, there are a few suppliers in the United States that occasionally import French varieties, notably the low alpha Strisselspalt, considered to have fine "noble" aromatics. UK Fuggle hops are a reasonable substitute with comparable earthy, aniseed (licorice) characteristics and a similarly moderate alpha acid content as compared to French Brewers Gold hops.

Bittering Charge

Bittering is in the range of 18 to 22 IBUs, preferably from French Brewers Gold or UK Fuggle hops. Exact extraction rates vary according to brew kettle geometry, heating methods, wort pH, and other factors.

In the following example we are targeting 18 IBUs using Brewers Gold hops (6.2% alpha acid) with a known alpha acid extraction efficiency of 30%.

Target bitterness of 18 IBUs (mg/l) with a 30% extraction rate requires that we add 18mg/0.3 or 60 mg/l alpha acid to the brew kettle.

At 6.2% alpha acid (Brewers Gold hops, 2003 crop) this means that we need to add 60mg/0.062 alpha or 967 mg (0.97 grams) Brewers Gold hops per liter of wort.

1 U.S. barrel = 117 liters (5 U.S. gallons = 18.7 liters)

This results in a hop bittering addition of Brewers Gold hops (6.2% alpha acids) of 0.97 grams x 117 liters which is equal to 113.5 grams/U.S. barrel or 4 ounces Brewers Gold hops per U.S. barrel.

0.25 lbs/U.S. barrel or 18 grams/5 U.S. gallons of Brewers Gold hops (6.2% alpha acid) to obtain 18 IBUs

Flavor/Aroma Hops

The use of clearly detectable flavor or aroma hops in *bière de garde* is uncommon but not inappropriate if kept at a low intensity, just above or near average threshold levels. In beer tasters' lingo, this hop aroma level might be described as "barely detectable" or "in the background." Low alpha, noble varieties are preferred with French Strisselspalt the obvious first choice. If Strisselspalt is not available, German-grown varieties such as Hallertauer Herzbrucker, Spalt, Tettnanger, or Czech Saaz will provide appropriately spicy, herbal character reminiscent of Alsatian Strisselspalt.

If a classic *bière de garde* character is desired it would be advisable to follow a more typical European approach to late hopping by allowing twenty to thirty minutes of boiling time after the late hop addition in order to obtain a faint spicy/herbal aroma and flavor. Less boiling time might yield a more pungent "grassy" aromatic that is not traditional but is a matter of personal choice for the brewer. The usual French approach is that any detectable hop aroma is seen as an accent or added dimension to malt-dominated aroma and flavor. If you wish to obtain a typical French *bière de garde* aroma profile it is advisable to use no late hop addition or to keep additions within the following guidelines:

- **Late hop addition (twenty to thirty minutes before end of boil)**
- **Using French Strisselspalt (2.1% alpha acid for 2003 crop)**

For a "barely detectable" aroma and flavor, a late hop rate of 0.10 to 0.12 pounds (1.6 to 2.0 ounces) per U.S. barrel might be considered appropriate. This translates to approximately 0.25 to 0.3 ounces (7.5 to 9.0 grams) per 5 U.S. gallons.

Note: At this hopping rate using French Strisselspalt (or German variety under 4% alpha acid), the amount of late hop bitterness contributed (at twenty to thirty minutes boiling time) would add only about 1.5 IBU to the final brew, a practically negligible amount.

Yeast

Yeast selection in modern French *bière de garde* is based primarily on choosing strains that produce clean, lager-like fermentations with no detectable diacetyl character. Many French *bière de garde* producers use a true ale strain (*Saccharomyces cerevisiae*) at lower temperatures than are typically used in Belgium and the UK, usually in the range of 66 to 68° F (18 to 20° C). There are several brewers who use lager yeast (*Saccharomyces uvarium*) at temperatures slightly higher than are typically used in traditional lager brewing. With either approach, there is the common goal of brewing a product with reduced (but not totally eliminated) fruity aromatics (esters) allowing for a purer expression of malt character. From this author's experience, German ale strains seem to perform more reliably than their traditional British counterparts at reduced temperatures. The German strains generally stay in suspension toward the end of fermentation and therefore tend to be more attenuative than many British yeasts that have a reputation for dropping out of suspension toward the end of fermentation when higher-order sugars (polysaccharides such as maltotriose) are encountered.

The choice to use lager yeasts may have come to be based on more proficient French brewers having been educated in lager beer production, therefore being more familiar with these yeasts, or possibly the result of small brewers not having the means to manage their own yeasts and getting whatever strains were available from larger, local breweries (almost all lager producers).

North American craft brewers and homebrewers have a wide range of different yeast strains available to them, thanks to two well-stocked domestic yeast labs. The following is a guide to some cultures (by no means the only choices) that are appropriate choices for *bière de garde* and are readily available from the two leading suppliers to the brewing community, Wyeast Labs Inc. and White Labs Inc.

Ale Yeasts

Many strains of ale yeast are appropriate choices for *bière de garde*. The typical modern approach uses neutral ale yeasts, often at a lower fermentation temperature to reduce but not necessarily eliminate ester formation. An "old world" option would be to use an estery yeast strain at typical ale fermentation temperatures (68 to 75° F, 20 to 24° C) as is done at Brasserie La Choulette and St. Sylvestre. Cold stabilizing the brew after primary fermentation (four to six weeks is typical) will tend to reduce some of the esters and bring out the smoothness that comes with extended cold storage.

The following ale strains are considered appropriate choices for *bière de garde* (listed in order of preference).

Recommended Ale Yeasts for Brewing Bière de Garde

WHITE LABS	Suggested Fermentation Temperature	Degree of Attenuation	Comments
WLP003 German Ale II	66-68° F (19-20° C)	73-80%	Clean, dry with minimal ester production.
WLP029 German Ale/Kölsch	64-66° F (18-19° C)	72-78%	Clean, "lager-like" profile. Low-med attenuation.
WLP011 European Ale	66-68° F (19-20° C)	65-70%	Produces fuller-bodied, malt-accented bière de garde.
WLP008 East Coast Ale	66-68° F (19-20° C)	70-75%	Use for slightly more fruity, winey character.
WLP001 American Ale	68-70° F (19-20° C)	73-80%	Classic, highly versatile American ale yeast (Ballantine, Narragansett).

Table 5. Recommended commercially available ale yeast strains for reproducing *bière de garde*.

Recommended Ale Yeasts for Brewing Bière de Garde cont.

WYEAST LABS	Suggested Fermentation Temperature	Degree of Attenuation	Comments
1338 European Ale	66-68° F (19-20° C)	67-71%	Produces fuller-bodied malt-accented *bière de garde.*
2565 Kölsch	64-66° F (18-19° C)	73-77%	Clean, "lager-like" profile. Low-med attenuation.
1007 German Ale	64-66° F (18-19° C)	73-77%	Clean, dry, very powdery yeast.
1010 American Wheat	65-68° F (18-20° C)	74-78%	Use for drier, fruity, winey character.
1056 American Ale	68-70° F (19-20° C)	73-77%	Classic highly versatile American ale yeast (Ballantine, Narragansett).

Table 6. Recommended commercially available ale yeast strains for reproducing *bière de garde.*

Modern bottling equipment in use for producing farmhouse ales.

Recommended Lager Yeasts for Brewing Bière de Garde

WHITE LABS	Suggested Fermentation Temperature	Degree of Attenuation	Comments
WLP830 German Lager	58-62° F (14-16° C)	74-79%	Workhorse European lager strain, clean, easy to use (low diacetyl).
WLP920 Old Bavarian	58-62° F (14-16° C)	66-73%	Popular lager strain, clean, low diacetyl production. Apple-like notes.
WLP810 SF Lager	62-65° F (16-18° C)	65-70%	User friendly, versatile yeast with "grape-like" ester production.

WYEAST LABS	Suggested Fermentation Temperature	Degree of Attenuation	Comments
2124 Bohemian Lager	58-62° F (14-16° C)	69-73%	Workhorse European lager strain, clean, easy to use (low diacetyl).
2007 Pilsen Lager	58-62° F (14-16° C)	71-75%	Popular lager strain, clean, low diacetyl production. Apple-like notes.
2112 California Lager	62-65° F (16-18° C)	67-71%	User friendly, versatile yeast with "grape-like" ester production.

Table 7. Recommended commercially available lager yeast strains for reproducing *bière de garde*.

SAMPLE RECIPES

Bière de Garde – Large Brewery Version

Malt Type	Color (ASBC)	Grist % by Weight
Pilsener	1.6	99.40%
Kiln Black	500	0.60%

Bittering Hops: 18-20 IBUs
Suggested Variety: Brewers Gold or Fuggle

Late Hop Addition (last 20-30 min. of boil)
1.5 oz./US bbl (7 grams/5 gal.)

Suggested Variety: Strisselspalt or Hallertauer

Options: Add up to 5% brown sugar (by extract)

Fermentation: Lager strain at 58-62° F

Secondary Storage: 3-4 weeks at 32-35° F

Original Gravity: 16 °P (1.064 SG)

Comments: In this approach the simple malt bill is dictated by difficulties of handling a variety of specialty malts in a large brewery. An extended boil (two to three hours) will add complexity and character. This grist formulation will yield a *bière de garde* suitable for longer-term storage (greater than six months).

Bière de Garde – Artisanal Brewery Version

Malt Type	Color (ASBC)	Grist % by Weight
Pilsener	1.6	75.0%
Munich	14	15.0%
Special Aromatic	4.5	5.0%
Amber/Biscuit	20	1.2%
Caramel Vienna	20	3.5%
Kiln Black	500	0.3%

Bittering Hops: 20-22 IBUs
Suggested Variety: Brewers Gold or Fuggle

Late Hop Addition (last 20-30 min. of boil)
2 oz./US bbl (9 grams/5 gal.)

Suggested Variety: Strisselspalt or Hallertauer

Options: Add up to 8% white sugar (by extract)

Fermentation: Ale strain at 66-68° F

Secondary Storage: 3-4 weeks at 32-35° F

Original Gravity: 17 °P (1.072 SG)

Comments: This artisanal version uses a variety of specialty malts to yield a greater complexity and depth of malt flavor. Hop additions are slight more aggressive as compared to the "large brewery" version and the original gravity is slightly higher to mirror a typical specialty brewer approach. Use of a neutral ale yeast at reduced temperature is suggested.

Bière de Mars

Malt Type	Color (ASBC)	Grist % by Weight
Pilsener	1.6	50.0%
Munich	14	14.8%
Wheat Malt	4.5	35.0%
Kiln Black	500	0.2%

Bittering Hops: 26-28 IBUs
Suggested Variety: Brewers Gold or Fuggle

Late Hop Addition (last 20 min. of boil)
2.5 oz./US bbl (12 grams/5 gal.)
Suggested Variety: Strisselspalt or Saaz

Finish Hop Addition (last 5 min. of boil)
4.25 oz/US bbl (20 grams/5 gal.)
Suggested Variety: Strisselspalt or Saaz

Options: Add up to 5% white sugar (by extract)

Fermentation: Ale strain at 64-66° F

Secondary Storage: 4-6 weeks at 32-35° F

Original Gravity: 15.5 ° P (1.066 SG)

Comments: This *bière de Mars* recipe emphasizes hop character over the typical French *bière de garde* ale. The use of a large proportion of wheat malt helps lend this brew a distinct "spring-like" quality. A long cold storage period adds an authentic lager-like smoothness.

Bière de Noel

Malt Type	Color (ASBC)	Grist % by Weight
Pilsener	1.6	70.0%
Munich	14	24%
Caramel Munich	60	5.5%
Kiln Black	500	0.5%

Bittering Hops: 22-24 IBUs
Suggested Variety: Brewers Gold or Fuggle

Late Hop Addition (last 20 min. of boil)
3 oz./US bbl (14 grams/5 gal.)
Suggested Variety: Strisselspalt or Hallertauer

Options: Add up to 10% brown sugar (by extract)

Fermentation: Ale strain at 66-68° F

Secondary Storage: 2-3 weeks at 32-35° F

Original Gravity: 18.5 ° P (1.074 SG)

Comments: Rich, complex malt character is the defining flavor in this French-style Christmas ale. A deep chestnut color and spicy, nutty malt notes emphasize the savory aspect of what many brewers consider to be their most special brew of the year.

Saison

six

A History of Saison
by Yvan De Baets

S aison beers represent one of the most difficult subjects for a brewing historian. They were essentially very local beers developed in farmhouse breweries, brewed only during part of the year and rarely distributed outside of their immediate region or even outside of their village. The recipes varied greatly from one brewery to another and very few written records exist for these beers. At most, one finds incomplete, sporadic references in brewing texts from the nineteenth century and first part of the twentieth century. It is those references, conversations with past and present *saison* brewers, and a contextualization of the brewing techniques and purposes of the ancient times that permit us to trace the general profile of these beers.

Tasting notes of *saisons* from breweries that have unfortunately disappeared have also helped to better define them. Furthermore, several breweries still produce them and fortunately these *saisons* are similar to those of the past.

The term *saison* refers to a type of beer that was once found in different brewing regions; they were beers destined for storage or keeping (*bières de garde*). They differed from beers brewed for immediate consumption, the majority of beers produced at that time.

Production conditions were the opposite of the aseptic ones, controlled from A to Z, that one finds in modern breweries. Brewing science was still in an embryonic stage. Pasteur's discoveries on fermentation in beer were published in 1876. It would take many years before their applications would become widespread, and they would first affect the large industrial breweries before the small local ones. Therefore most beers became infected quickly and were drunk quite young—approximately one to three weeks after production. It was almost out of the question to brew in the summer, a period extremely vulnerable to infections that would have made the beer undrinkable. Brewers needed to make a beer that would keep for the warm season.

Spontaneous fermentation was originally used to make beer, most likely since at least the Mesolithic era (10,000 years ago) and most certainly since the Neolithic period. Little by little, man (or more accurately woman, since women were the only ones found to be pure enough to brew beer, the drink of the gods) learned to reuse the yeast from previous fermentation in order to start the next batch. However, the conditions under which beer was made couldn't prevent the development of wild yeasts and bacteria. All fermentations were therefore inevitably  "mixed" (aside from lambic, which was exclusively an adaptation of spontaneous fermentation).

As time went on, empiricism and the talent of certain brewers allowed them to make beers that kept longer. For this they relied on lactic along with mixed fermentation that, thanks to the production of lactic acid by certain wild bacteria, provided these beers with a natural preservative that lengthened their life considerably. The gradual lowering of the beer's pH caused by lactic acid released in the medium checked the development of unwanted bacteria. Furthermore, the lactic acid along with the aromatic compounds produced by certain wild yeasts gave the beer a pleasing nose. Of course, the importance of brewing during the colder months was well known for ages and this contributed heavily to limiting major infections.

Brewers also realized that the addition of certain aromatics not only helped in the conservation of the beer but also improved its flavor. Hops were most likely chosen initially for their bacteriostatic properties that are higher than other spices. Ever since their use in brewing (in the eighth and ninth centuries), brewers recommended using them in quantities necessary to produce longer-lasting beers.

A third factor known to help in the conservation of beer consisted of brewing beers with a higher than average gravity since alcohol was a preservative. Stored beers were therefore heavier than other beers. It is necessary however to look at the average gravity of beers of the period in order to understand what is meant by the term "strong beer." If we take the average alcohol percentage of the Belgian beers in the nineteenth century, according to Mulder[1], it was in the vicinity of 3% alcohol by volume—and this is without taking in to account the household or table beers, which are even lower in alcohol. A beer with 4% abv was then considered a relatively strong beer.

The evolution of this empirical knowledge led to the development of beers for keeping, most likely simultaneously in the different brewing regions: in Germany, where L. Figuier[2] places their origins in the twelfth century; in Great Britain (stock ales, stout, porter); in northern France[3]; and, of course, in Belgium. However, those kind of beers certainly go all the way back to Sumeria.

In Belgium, each region had its own beer for keeping. In Brussels, there was *lambic* and its derivatives; in Flanders, in the region of Ghent, *Double Uytzet*; in Antwerp, *L'Orge d'Anvers* (*Gerst* in Dutch); later, in the region of Roulers, the red beers of Flanders appeared, and in the region of Oudenaarde, the *oud bruin* (old brown). In Wallonia, they had *saison*[4].

THE ORIGIN OF SAISON

It is important to emphasize that *saison* doesn't constitute a type but rather a family of special beers. *Saisons* originated in Wallonia, in southern Belgium, with an important concentration in the province of Hainaut. Nevertheless, several Flemish beers can be considered to be close to *saison* as well.

Saisons were brewed at the beginning of winter in a farmhouse brewery in order to quench the thirst of the farmhands who worked in the fields in the summer. The *saisons* that were brewed in the winter had to survive the spring without becoming too infected. Sometimes these beers were called *saisons d'été* or summer *saisons*[5].

Each brewer had his own recipe and it is thus difficult to attribute a precise flavor profile or brewing method to the style. However, all shared certain general characteristics that connected them to "the family."

It is also a type of beer that has undergone an evolution over time, both through improved techniques and the tastes of the consumer. The period following World War II marked an important turning point in their production.

It is impossible to say exactly when the beer style was born. It seems logical, however, that its origin goes back to the beginning of agriculture, when quenching, nourishing beers were essential to getting the fieldwork done, making *saison*, in a way, a multimillennial beer. At harvest time, larger farms would hire outside labor called seasonal workers (*les saisonniers*). The exhausting work in the fields, often in the sun, made the workers very thirsty. They needed a drink that was fortifying and refreshing and not too high in alcohol content. From a hygienic standpoint, this beverage also needed to be safe, and often water was questioned as a possible source of infection. Beer, refreshing because of its low alcohol content (in those days at least), invigorating due to the different spices (hops or otherwise) used to flavor it, and safe due to the boiling of the wort during the brewing process, fulfilled all of these conditions.

Based on the works of sociologist and historian Léo Moulin[6], it can be estimated that consumption levels of low gravity beer for a manual laborer in the Middle Ages was around 5 liters per day! And this is just a yearly average that undoubtedly increased considerably in the summer. In those days, therefore, beer made up the main intake of water for workers. The farmers needed to have a sufficient amount of beer for the summer, simply to ensure that work got done.

Brewing *saisons* also served to provide work for the year-round workers in the winter, and to produce spent grain that served as quality feed for livestock.

Note that these farms would have been rather large-scale; the fact that they had a brewery, even a small one, and employed a large amount of labor in the summer suggests that they were culturally important for the times. The small farmers who didn't have the means to own a brewery gathered together to brew their *saison* in a village brewery, or later a communal brewery if one existed[7], so that they, too, could have beer during harvest time. This practice is confirmed by Marc Rosier; until the first half of the twentieth century, it was common for the village farmers to go two or three at a time to a neighbor's brewery in the winter so that they could prepare a reserve of *saison* for the following summer. After brewing, they would return home with casks to ferment and mature in their own cellars.

CHARACTERISTICS

To get an idea of the profile of early *saisons*, it is necessary to look at the purpose of such a beer and the production conditions at the time.

As previously mentioned, *saisons* were meant to be refreshing. Therefore, it is wrong to imagine a syrupy brown beer of 10% alcohol. Rather, *saisons* were pale and light in alcohol and flavor. They were often sour and/or bitter in flavor.

According to R. Pinon[8], in certain regions of Wallonia there were only two specific times for brewing *saisons*: in December, during Advent (the beers were therefore called *bière des Avents*) and in March, since these were periods of rest for farmers. In other regions, they were brewed only in November. These events were celebrated as special occasions by the farm families.

According to J. Cartuyvels and Ch. Stammer[9], the provision beers (i.e. the beers to be kept) of Hainaut were brewed from December to March to be drunk from May to September. However, the brewers probably let them age even longer. According to Jean-Louis Dits, documents pertaining to the management of barrels at the old Biset-Cuvelier brewery (now Brasserie Vapeur) show that some *saisons* were consumed after a year-and-a-half to two years of storage. Some of these beers were still very rough after only several months of maturing. A longer aging time softened the edges. According to G. M. Johnson[10], "young, these beers naturally were not drinkable; however, the bitterness disappeared little by little and one knows that heavy doses of hops increased the conservation quality of beers and preserved their flavor when they aged."

RAW MATERIALS

Many different types of raw materials could be used in the composition of *saisons*. Generally it depended on what the brewer had on hand.

Farmhouse breweries usually grew their own barley and malted it themselves. At the time, malting equipment and knowledge didn't always allow them to obtain the pale malt that we know today. Basic pale malt, unevenly kilned, was somewhat amber in color, a fact confirmed by Cartuyvels and Stammer[11]: "The kilns used were generally somewhat primitive and defective, using direct heat or a heating chamber; the grain stayed in the kiln for only twenty-four hours; it was subjected to a temperature of 60 to 70° C (140 to 158° F); it was almost always lightly amber and glazed." Initially, the malt was not germinated for long, which meant that the acrospire grew to only half the length of the grain[12].

The authors noted a later use of malt that had been germinated for a longer period and that was kilned slowly with much ventilation for three to four days, reaching a temperature of approximately 80 to 100° C (176 to 212° F) during the final twenty-four hours[13]. This was made possible by advancements in the malting process.

The barley that was used and recommended was a six-row winter barley (escourgeon) commonly cultivated in those days. This barley, according to Cartuyvels and Stammer, was the malt "typical of the Wallonian country," contained much nitrogenous material (which deepens the color of the malt during kilning) and husk, rich in polyphenols (which deepen the color of the wort during brewing, by oxidation). These two factors gave *saisons* a certain acridness, says Claude Allard. Winter barley did not allow for the brewing of refined beers, giving *saisons* a rustic character.

Malted barley wasn't necessarily the only grain used to brew *saisons*. Many brewers often used wheat as well as oats, buckwheat, and especially spelt that was eventually malted. The proportions used varied greatly, and sometimes the other grains were used in a greater proportion than the barley itself. Traditionally they were grown by the farmhouse brewers and were less expensive than malted barley. They contributed a pale color to the beer and also added to the refreshing character by giving it a certain smoothness. In addition, some of the grains, like wheat, were reputed to improve the "vinosity" of the beers, something that was very sought after. Vinosity refers to the very complex flavors found in Jerez and sherry wines, for instance. It includes a "wild yeast" estery flavor, some woodiness, and eventually an apple-like aroma coming from the oxidative fermentation.

Brasserie Ellezeloise is a tiny farm brewery that produces a revivalist saison.

The unusual square fermenters at Brasserie Dupont are said to be a factor in the unique character of its ales.

Pierre and Vinciane Delcoigne are the young, energetic owners of Brasserie des Geants, an upstart brewery that has revived an old local favorite, Saison Voisin.

Brouwerij Kerkom is said to be the oldest continuously operating farm brewery in Belgium. It is located in northeast corner of Flanders close to the Dutch border.

In the Old World the town church and the brewery are never far apart; in the foreground is the brewhouse of Brasserie St. Sylvestre.

Michel (left) and Armand Theillier are the present and former brewmasters at Brasserie Theillier (Armand is still active in selling the beer).

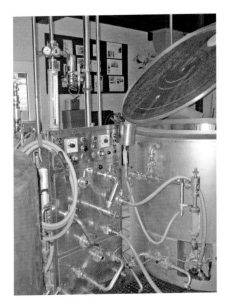

Some small farm breweries are surprisingly high-tech: (above) the computerized brew-house at Brasserie Bailleux; (below) the modern bottling line at Brasserie St. Sylvestre.

Brewmaster Serge Ricour (above) and his brother Pierre run Brasserie St. Sylvestre, a brewery started by their grandfather in the 1920s.

Alain Dhaussy checks a brew at Brasserie LaChoulette, a classic farm brewery located in the French Department du Nord.

Franconia, the northern portion of Bavaria, is home to hundreds of small farm breweries; unfortunately, the original ale styles that were once brewed have been lost. Shown above is Brauerie Ibel, in the town of Kappel in western Franconia.

The eastern end of Long Island, New York where the author lives and works has a long tradition of farming. Here Phil shares a saison with fourth generation Southampton farmer (and homebrewer) Mark Corwith.

The tasting room at Brasserie Thiriez is filled with memorabilia that illustrates the rich brewing history of French Flanders.

Brewmaster Daniel Thiriez (left) discussing (and sampling) beer with Yvan De Baets in the tasting room at Brasserie Thiriez.

Brewmaster Marie-Noelle Pourtois removes spent grain from a batch of Saison d'Epeautre at Brasserie Blaugies.

Brasserie Dupont is a quintessential farm brewery located in the peaceful village of Tourpes in Hainaut province.

According to Cartuyvels and Stammer, an average malt bill consisted of 20 to 28 kilos of grain per 160-liter tun (barrel). Keep in mind that extract efficiency of the malt of the period was less than what it is today.

Around 1900, an average density of 4 to 5 °Belgian before fermentation is often cited, which corresponds to 10.3 and 12.7 °Plato or (1.040 or 1.050 OG). Prior to 1900, the gravity was around 7 to 9 °Plato or 1,025 to 1.036 OG. Later, it would rise to around 1.057 OG, or 14 °Plato.

Saisons, like all stored beers, were generally heavily hopped[14]. The bacteriostatic properties of hops protected the beer from unwanted infections. Cartuyvels and Stammer[15] mention the use of an average of 500 to 800 grams of hops per hectoliter, of which one-third was added at the end of the boil. However, they also say that the "quantity varies in each

village" and it is therefore probable that some *saisons* were rather lightly hopped. It is well understood that Belgian hops, traditionally grown in the province of Hainaut, were most often used since they were grown near the brewery and were the most readily available. At the beginning of the twentieth century, German or English hops, if available, would sometimes be used as aroma hops at the end of the boil.

It is important to note that the alpha acid content of hops at the time was 2 to 4% on average. They therefore contributed proportionally less bitterness. On the other hand, Belgian hops were of poorer quality than their German or British counterparts and gave the beer a rather harsh bitterness.

It should also be noted that the high hopping rate is not at all incompatible with the sourness of the beers nor will it prevent their eventual acidification. This acidification occurred in most cases and was considered a desirable quality, confirmed Mulder[16]. According to him, lactic acid "was found in all beers". He mentions Belgian beers in particular.

It is likely that when the brewer wished to produce a *saison* with a predominant sourness, he would use a greater proportion of old hops so as not to contribute too much bitterness and to encourage the development of lactic bacteria. Farmhouse breweries would most likely have a stock of old or imperfectly stored hops on hand. The use of older hops was frequent, bringing *saisons* close to traditional lambic.

The practice of dry hopping was widespread for stored beers in general and for *saisons* in particular. It was intended to rejuvenate old beers before the barrels were sent to the consumer. It could also have been performed at the start of the conditioning period. Johnson[17] explains that "these hops were covered with wild yeasts and bacteria which, without a doubt, helped to give a special character to the beer due to their work during the secondary fermentation." The pre-scribed measure was around 100 grams of raw hops (the best quality possible) per hectoliter of beer[18] but that amount could increase to up to 400 grams[19]. *Saison* Dupont benefited from dry hopping until the 1960s.

Hops were not the only spice used to flavor *saisons*. Star anise, sage, coriander, green peppercorns, cumin, orange peel, and ginger were used. Ginger in particular appeared frequently—as did star anise—for its refreshing contribution to the beer's taste but also for its preservation characteristics[20]. As with the other raw materials, the brewer used whatever he had on hand, and not all *saisons* were spiced. However, it seems that most of them were until World War II and some still are today. The Dupont Brewery abandoned the use of spices in its *saison* in the 1960s. According to Marc Rosier, more spices were used when the hops were of just average quality.

One rule of thumb is nonetheless applied to their use: moderation! Spices are present in *saisons* in order to subtly enhance their flavor. Ideally, one shouldn't be able to detect them individually.

The water of western Hainaut is hard, containing high levels of bicarbonates and sulfates. Bicarbonates are sometimes responsible for a rather harsh bitterness, depending on the type of hops that are used; sulfates contribute a very dry quality to the beers. These characteristics were nevertheless balanced by wine-like qualities.

A frequent question about *saison* water revolves around its iron content, with some people claiming that there is an "obligation" for a *saison* to have an iron-like taste. As is usual for this beer, there is no specific rule here. In some villages, water has a high iron level, in others, very low, depending on the nature of the soil. For instance, in Tourpes (Dupont), there is no iron, but in Leuze, lots of it, despite the fact that the villages are only 5 kilometers apart.

In some old *saisons*, like the *Extra Vieille* from Allard-Groetenbril, the ancient *Saison Voisin* and the *Saison de Pipaix*, one could find an iron-like taste. Its origin was not the water but the brewing equipment: those three breweries (Allard-Groetenbril and Voisin having since closed) had very old brewing equipment, including old lagering tanks of iron. Some (almost all) were damaged and rusty, which explains the iron-like taste in their beers. This problem has been solved at Pipaix, so that the iron taste of the *saison* comes from the water and is lower than before. But there is not at all any obligation for a *saison* to have that taste. Note that a too-high iron content in brewing water (0.3 mg/l or more) can be a significant problem for brewers, as it is harmful to yeast.

BREWING TECHNIQUES

Brewing was done by infusion since initially that was the most commonly used method in Belgium. Even after the widespread use of decoction, infusion remained the rule—farmhouse breweries generally used rudimentary equipment that wasn't suitable for decoction.

Mash in was done at 40° C[21]. It is hard to get a precise idea of the brewing schedule of the era and its consequence on the production of fermentable sugars in the wort. Malt was very different from what we are familiar with today and had a lower yield. It appears that the goal was the production of the highest amount possible of fermentable sugars. The creation of a more dextrinous wort wouldn't have posed a problem, however; the dextrins served as nutrients for the secondary wild yeasts and bacteria (see the "Fermentation" section). Brewers desiring a sour *saison* would have brewed more dextrinous worts to encourage the development of these wild fermentations that perfected the beer's attenuation. Those who didn't want such tartness would produce worts made entirely of malt with a high percentage of fermentable sugars and with much hopping[22].

Worts varied greatly from one brewery to another but the final result was always a highly attenuated beer. Note that M.

Jackson as well as R. Protz mention that *saisons* contain unfermentable sugars. They apparently are referring to the *saison de Liège*, a specific type of beer that has completely disappeared today and which did have unfermentable sugars (see previous). It is possible that certain current brewers who make a similar *saison* confirmed this to them, in order to justify their syrupy products. But it is clear that the "true" *saisons* don't have many residual sugars, their attenuation being extraordinarily high.

The third runnings would often be used to make a *bière de ménage* or a *bière de table* (household or table beer), very low in alcohol (from 0.8 to 1.2% abv on average). The two were certainly mixed to make *saison*, since those farm breweries didn't brew a wide range of beers. A wider range appeared when they ceased farming and became dedicated breweries after World War II.

The boil lasted for five to eight hours and sometimes up to fifteen hours "due to the generally accepted opinion that beer kept better the longer it was boiled."[23] This resulted in a deeper colored wort, intensified by the fact that the copper boiling kettles were generally heated by open fire. In addition, it was

common to add lime to the boiling kettle to artificially deepen the color of the wort. This practice was denounced early in the brewing literature[24], but it seems it was sometimes used until the early twentieth century.

Since they were by essence artisanal, *saisons* were not filtered, were brewed in small batches, and were unpasteurized, even after the use of this method for the preservation of beer around the 1860s[25].

FERMENTATION OF SAISONS

By necessity, *Saisons* were top fermenting since this was the only type of fermentation used until the twentieth century in small Belgian breweries. Even after the development of bottom fermenting yeast it was still the norm, as these small breweries were most definitely not equipped for that type of fermentation. Note also that *saisons* are always mentioned in brewing books under the chapter "top fermentation." Top fermentation evolved into a mixed fermentation because a spontaneous culture coexisted with the top fermenting yeast. This was caused by production conditions: chilling the wort in shallow cool ships, fermentation and conditioning in unpitched wooden casks, and brewing on a farm. Emil Hansen perfected the technique of culturing pure yeasts in 1883. It would be years before it was applied by commercial breweries. It would be even longer before it came to the farmhouse breweries, which later became small village breweries where the equipment was reduced to the bare minimum. Until the 1950s, the yeast most frequently used was a mix of several different yeast strains, some of which were wild, as well as containing lactic and/or other bacteria. The yeast was reused from batch to batch.

Marc H. Van Laer[26] says that, "in stored beers, secondary fermentation is attributed to the special yeasts that possess a higher level of attenuation than that of the primary yeasts." He specifies that by that time (1942), it was possible to artificially produce such a mixture that confirms that the yeast originally used contained wild strains. This is still the case at the Dupont

Brewery where the yeast is composed of several different strains, including at least one or more wild yeasts that are highly attenuative. These "secondary" yeasts have the property to hydrolyze and then ferment certain dextrins. In order that the primary yeast could work and contribute its characteristics to the beer, the secondary yeast couldn't be too prominent at the beginning of fermentation or possess a high growth rate. Van Laer also indicates that the secondary yeasts "create rather high amounts of organic acids which slowly turn the alcohol into esters and cause the appearance of the wine-like taste characteristic of old beers." This is confirmed by correspondence with Léon Voisin, retired brewer of the old Voisin Brewery in Flobecq (Saison Voisin), who confirms this character of old *saisons* as does A. Laurent[27]. Van Laer adds that "the most typical common strains of these secondary yeasts were also found in spontaneously fermented beers."

It is interesting to note that as early as 1920, Van Laer criticized the phenomenon, almost completely widespread today, of simplifying the organoleptic qualities of beers by fermenting them only with "pure" yeast strains[28]. "It is certain that the introduction of pure yeasts into industrial fermentations does not constitute the crowning achievement of a system that is henceforth immutable. It seems, for example, that if the application of the pure cultures method has improved the average quality of the beer, if it has decreased the chances of infection, it has given us beer with less character than before."

It should be clarified that Van Laer did not categorically oppose the technique of pure yeast culturing, but specified that it was being used in a narrow and extreme fashion, causing the elimination of a number of organisms that contributed to the aromatic richness of Belgian beers. The current situation of

Belgian beer, some having become caricatures of themselves with their mainstream, standardized flavors, shows us that, unfortunately, Van Laer's warning was not heeded.

Brewers of *saison*, like most brewers, reused their yeast from batch to batch. When a major infection occurred, Rosier and Allard report that the brewer would borrow his neighbor's strain. This yeast would adapt to its new environment, allowing each brewery to keep its unique characteristics. Moreover, according to Allard, it would frequently happen that the yeast would simply become tired when pitched into a weak wort that was deficient in nutrients. The brewer would then ask his neighbor to use that yeast once or twice in his own wort in order to revive it. In addition, a brewer who particularly liked the character of another brewery's beer would culture the yeast from the dregs of a bottle.

It is also likely that some brewers of *saison* used only spontaneous fermentation for their beers. In fact, there is a mention in *Petit Journal du Brasseur* in 1913[29] of an "unfermented *bière de garde*" aged for one to two years before being delivered to the customer. In a later edition that also addresses this subject, it is noted that this phrase does indeed refer to spontaneous fermentation; therefore, they are obviously not referring to a brewer of lambic.

Up until World War I, the majority of *saisons* were fermented in unpitched wooden barrels that held an average of 150 to 200 liters. They were unpitched "in the kind that will leave all its flavor with the old beer."[30]

According to Lacambre[31], conditioning in barrels was done at warmer temperatures in the winter (28 to 30 °C) than in spring or fall (24 to 25 °C). Primary fermentation took place at 18 to 25 °C.

After primary fermentation, either in a metallic (*guilloire*) vat or in a cask, the beer was decanted into other casks kept in a cool cellar. Sometimes brewers who didn't have cellars large enough to hold all of their casks "would requisition all the spacious cellars [of the village] in order to age their beer."[32] The barrels were filled to the rim in order to assure the best possible saturation of carbon dioxide. Topping off took place at the beginning of fermentation. Secondary fermentation would have been slow and "good and cold," which is to say between 10 and 15 °C for top fermenting beers. The goal of fermenting at a lower temperature was to obtain a slow fermentation in order to provide the beer with supplemental protection and refine its flavor[33]. Clarification would have been obtained through natural decanting and not by fining or other procedure—except in the case of a production mistake[34].

Given the relative control that the brewer of *saison* had over the fermentation of his beer, it sometimes happened that it would turn too sour, in part because of the presence of acetic bacteria. According to Allard, one of the methods used to counteract sourness was to add crushed eggshells to the beer.

Note that the use of metallic fermentation tanks was developed between the two World Wars but that their general implementation took time, especially in the small breweries where their use was sporadic.

After maturating, the beer was shipped to the customer. It could be served flat almost like a lambic and it seems that this was often the case, at least early on.

Brewers could carbonate the beer in two ways: either add a bit of Havana sugar—also known as cane sugar—or candi sugar that caused refermentation in the barrel, or add young beer taken from the beginning of fermentation during the development phase of the yeast. J.-B. Bauby called this kraüsen "referment."[35] A little over 5 liters per hectoliter was added in order to referment old beers, sometimes reaching up to 10%[36]. Barrels were filled to the bunghole over three or four days, then were bunged, to be decanted in twenty-four to thirty-six hours. If the beer had to be shipped far, kegs containing between 25 and 75 liters were used. The kraüsen was added and they were hermetically sealed. When they arrived at their destination, they would rest for four to five days before being tapped. This technique wasn't used frequently in farmhouse breweries, however, or at least not initially, since they weren't brewing at the time of year when *saisons* were being drunk. Later, this technique could have been spread when the farmhouse breweries became only breweries.

Another technique used frequently in Belgium was the blending of beers. This technique appears to have been used with *saisons*[37] although, according to Cartuyvels and Stammer, it was not widespread in Hainaut[38]. A beer for storing—a *saison*, for example—would be brewed. Called "old beer," it would be matured for almost a year or longer (from seven months to two years, it appears). This extremely sour old beer was added to a young beer that had been brewed in March or April by a farmhouse brewery or even in summer by a regular brewery. The young beer was lightly hopped in order not to impart too much bitterness to the mixture and so that it wouldn't compete with the acidity brought by the old beer[39]. On average the proportions were one-quarter young beer to three-quarters old beer but they could vary greatly from one brewery to another. Refermentation would take place after several days in the cask, giving the beer a harmonious taste and blending of aromas. The old beer improved the young one by giving it vinous qualities and refreshing tartness as well as protection against bacterial infections. The young beer contributed freshness and carbonation and eventually allowed for the lowering of the alcohol tax to the desired level if it was a weaker beer.

Lambic was often used as a blending beer. Some lambic producers sold it almost exclusively for this purpose. Sometimes blending was done with vinegar or even, in some cases, with pure acetic acid. Tartaric acid was also used[40]. This proves that consumers at the time, at least in the regions of northern France and Belgium, were attracted by the sour flavor.

Saison was sometimes delivered to the fields in small kegs but was also brought to the workers in stoneware pitchers that helped to keep the beer cool. Later, *saison* was also delivered in bottles. According to Rosier, before World War II it was customary for the farmers to take the bottles with them and keep them in a hole dug at the edge of the field in order to keep them cool. They would unearth them during breaks to slake their thirst.

Kegs were also sent to taverns that sold *saison* (serving it in jugs) as well as to private individuals. At the Biset-Cuvelier Brewery (now Brasserie Vapeur), according to Jean-Louis Dits, the casks of *saison* (made of wood and containing 30 liters) were delivered to the private customers up until 1962. The customers then restarted the fermentation in different ways by "preparing" the beer. The consumption of *saison* both in the fields and in taverns coexisted for many years if not centuries. Most likely, the beer for the seasonal workers was more dilute in order not to incur a high alcohol tax while the beer destined for the taverns was stronger. Two grades of *saison* would have coexisted until around the time of World War I: a stronger, high quality *saison*—a Wallonian version of a top quality storage beer *(bière fine de conserve)*—drunk after the work day; and an everyday *(courante) saison* destined for the farmhands that would be diluted by a very weak or household beer, making the alcohol range from 2 to 2.5% abv or less.

Auguste Laurent, in his *Dictionnaire de Brasserie*[41] in 1875, distinguishes, without much precision, different categories of beers for keeping: a high quality storage beer that was stronger and aged in large tuns and considered to be a premium beer *(bière de conserve)*; old beer *(vieille bière)* that was less strong but aged longer in large barrels; and *saison,* that one could suppose was even weaker, aged "in regular barrels." *Saison* was presented therefore as a third-rate beer. It is probable that these distinctions were based on beers produced in breweries of different sizes and levels of technology. Beers for storage were therefore

CONTENU: 33 CL.   R.C. MONS 9657

Vieille Saison
Colmant

CUVÉE RÉSERVÉE   BIÈRE DE LUXE

made in the large industrial breweries of the time while *saisons* were made in farmhouse breweries that were inevitably not as well-equipped and therefore produced harsher beers. It is also possible that the author based his information on a range of beers brewed in the same brewery, wishing to distinguish between the different products. This distinction isn't found later on and it seems that it was between the two Wars when *saison* beers acquired the same premium reputation as the *bières de conserve*.

THE EVOLUTION OF SAISON:
THE TURNING POINT OF THE 1920s

Little by little, the farmhouse breweries disappeared. The progress of mechanization rendered the demand for seasonal workers superfluous. Activities became specialized; depending on the case either agricultural activity or brewing activity remained. According to Rosier, the last farmhouse breweries disappeared completely after World War II. In terms of beers produced, only the high quality *saisons* survived.

This trend actually started toward the end of the nineteenth century and increased greatly after World War I. Belgian brewers were confronted with the relentless competition of foreign beers: British pale ales, stouts, and, especially, bottom fermenting beers from Bavaria. These had a strong influence on the consumer who quickly became accustomed to their softer taste, lighter color, clarity, shelflife, and especially their consistency. In addition, these beers were of a slightly higher gravity than the Belgian ones.

Actually, the legislation of the nineteenth century favored the brewing of weaker beers. It was the size of the mash tun that determined the level of taxation. The mash tuns of the period were therefore ridiculously small and overloaded with cereals by the brewer. The spent grains were rinsed many times in order to remove the maximum of extract. The beers were therefore, on average, of a very weak gravity. The literature of the period[42] was full of advice for the government to change that law and for the brewers to modify their brewing techniques to produce higher gravity beers that had the qualities consumers sought. Of course, this advice wasn't followed in a uniform fashion by all brewers. Many old methods would endure for years.

At the same time, bottling of beer was also developing. Belgian brewers decided to fight the growing influence of foreign beers by proposing true "specialties" to the customers. They aimed for higher gravity beers and bottled them, often refermenting them in the bottle with the addition of sugar and yeast. Another practice, certainly more anecdotal, was used for refermentation in the bottle: some brewers added several grains of wheat or barley to each bottle in order to increase fermentation[43]. It was at this time as well (in the 1920s) that advertising for Belgian beers developed, with an emphasis on the national origin of these beverages.

Most of the time, brewers would base the recipe on an existing beer but increase the gravity. They also made an effort to obtain more consistent beers, using new techniques like fermenting in tanks and with pure yeast cultures, for example. *Saisons* also followed this evolution. However, because of their village origin, their evolution took longer than that of other beers. Fermentation in wooden casks continued longer than elsewhere as did the use of several yeast strains, including wild yeasts, which permitted them to keep their character for a longer period of time[44]. Their gravity increased, however, reaching about 10 to 14 °Plato (giving the beers an alcohol level ranging from 5 to a little bit less than 7% by volume, but no more since the beer needed to keep its refreshing aspect). Their reputation increased as well. One also saw the growth of *saisons* refermented in bottles, *bières de provision* (stock beers) that could be stored, and thus conditioned, for a long time in the cellars of the publicans or the consumers.

Little by little, with the improvement of brewing techniques that limited the risk of infection, *saisons* could be brewed year-round. The conditioning period was shortened, even if it was still longer on average than for other beers. Their second life in bottles was assured by the addition of sugar and fresh yeast during bottling. This development started before World War II and continues to this day.

It is important to note that in Belgium, the term *bière de garde* is used only in the brewing literature. It never appeared on labels or in advertising for the beers. In Wallonia, the beers were designated only by the term *"saison,"* sometimes matched with the adjective "old" (*vieille*, for example *Vieille Saison* from the Colmant Brewery) or even "old stock" (*Vieille Provision*, formerly on *Saison* Dupont labels). Sometimes one would find only the adjective "old" (Danhaive Brewery) which eventually ended up being the name of the beer (*Extra Vieille* from the Saint-Joseph Brewery). New marketing standards have completely eliminated this adjective that was once a mark of quality and a sign that a beer was brewed with the utmost care.

Saison was a well-renowned beer before World War II and each Wallonian brewery would have had one in its lineup. The traditional *saison* bottle is a 75 cl Champagne-style bottle that, according to Voisin, is a logical extension for a beer with a vinous character. Like traditional gueuze, it was necessary to have a bottle that could support significant pressure due to the refermentation of these highly attenuated beers.

The development in favor of higher gravity beers took place after World War II. Many *saisons* served as the basis for the conception of special, stronger beers, some of which are still on the market. *La Moinette* from the Dupont Brewery is one of these beers. In 1954, Sylva Rosier, the father of Marc Rosier, decided to create an "improved" *saison*, which meant, in the language of the time, a high gravity *saison*. He based the beer on the recipe for *Saison Dupont* and created *L'Abbaye de la Moinette*, a type of "super *saison*" containing 8.5% abv. Many other breweries followed suit.

THE ORGANOLEPTIC PROFILE OF OLD SAISONS
The general profile of old *saisons* would have revolved around the following nuances, although with numerous variations. It was traced, theoretically, by the aforementioned historians, and interpreted thanks to the fantastic experiences of tasting bygone *saisons*: among others, those of the Biset-Cuvelier Brewery in Pipaix, Voisin in Flobecq, and the *Extra Vieille* from the Saint-Joseph Brewery in Guignies.

- Their color was light for the period, which is to say more amber. With the evolution in malting techniques, the color eventually became somewhat lighter.
- Initially they were not highly carbonated but were rather flat. *Saisons* with a dense and creamy head appeared later, once they were bottled.
- As to the flavor, depending on the circumstances (the

presence of a more or less controlled infection, more or fewer hops, and aging), they would have had either a dominant sourness (primarily lactic, although sometimes a little acetic), which seems to have been found in the majority of the cases[45], or a dominant bitterness, with a sour side nonetheless.

- Initially the effect of the hops would have been to regulate rather than prevent infection. It is often said that sourness and bitterness do not go well together in beer but, because it was a beer that had matured for a long time, the bitterness decreased, permitting the equilibrated development of the sour and vinous flavors in the beer. We had evidence of this until several years ago when the excellent *XX Bitter*, a heavily hopped beer from the De Ranke Brewery in Wevelgem, was still fermented with yeast from the Rodenbach Brewery in Roeselare. This yeast is in fact a mix of diverse yeasts, some of which are of the *Brettanomyces* strain, and of lactic bacteria. When the beer was young, bitterness predominated, balanced by a light tartness. As it aged, the bitterness diminished, giving way to a more pronounced and lightly vinous tartness. The balance of this beer was always perfect. It certainly came very close to old *saison* beers.

- With the development in brewing techniques, some brewers gradually obtained a less infected *saison* that was therefore less sour. The dominant flavor of those *saisons* was bitterness (the evolution of *Saison Dupont* after World War II corresponds to this phenomenon) but sour *saisons* remained until the 1980s.

- An important characteristic was their wine-like character, a sign of aged beers that were properly made. This vinous and sour side corresponds, according to Laurent[46], to the "taste of the North" (Belgium and northern France), and was the "must have" of the era. The nose of old *saisons* was clearly marked by *Brettanomyces*. Notes of "old barrel" were also present.

- Note that the sour and vinous character of *saisons* brought them much closer to traditional gueuzes. This is confirmed by W. Belgeonne[47], who compares, in 1946, gueuzes to old Wallonian *saisons*! The tasting of old saisons absolutely confirms this.

- They were very well attenuated.

- Subtle spicy nuances appeared in some of them. A citrusy aroma from hops could also be present.

- Their fruity aspect was also subtle and non-predominant. An apple flavor was frequently encountered, from oxidative fermentation in barrels.

- Mouthfeel was dry and astringent. However, the use of wheat could contribute mellowness.

- The fact that they were not filtered gave them a well-rounded character.

- The alcohol level was around 3 to 3.5% abv on average initially and later increased to between 4.5 and 6.5%.

- The fact that *saison* beers do not correspond to a well-defined recipe can bother the modern brewer. A multitude of different raw materials can enter into their composition and many techniques can be used in their fabrication.

Allard was correct in saying that with *saisons,* "all whims are permitted." Of course this doesn't mean that anything goes, which is seen all too often today in Belgium. A *saison* doesn't belong to this authentic family of beers unless it respects certain characteristics connected with its purpose and history.

- A *saison* must therefore be low in alcohol (in the modern— and Belgian—sense of the word in any case), around 4.5 to 6.5%. It must be highly attenuated (90 to 95% on average, if not more, as apparent attenuation) and dry. It must also be either sour or very bitter (with a bitterness obtained by the use of a massive amount of hops low in alpha acid). It shouldn't in any case be smooth. If spices are used, it must be with the utmost moderation. A *saison* is not by any means a spice soup. Ideally, it should be fermented, at least partially, by wild yeasts as well as by cultured varieties. An authentic *saison* has a small "wild" side, rustic, indefinable, far from the clean aspect of certain engineered beers of today. In one word, it must have an extraordinary character.

Some beers brewed today are true authentic *saisons* even if their brewers do not always call them by that name. All of these beers offer great aromatic complexity and give an idea of the range of flavor and tastes that one would have found in these beers. These include the wonderfully complex *Saison Dupont* (of which there is also an organic version that offers different notes compared to the "classic") as an example of the bitter version; the *Biolégère,* also from the Dupont Brewery, for the light in alcohol version (3.5% abv); the *Saison d'Epeautre* (spelt) and the *Darbyste* from the Blaugies Brewery (fermented with prune juice), for the sour raw grain version; and the *Saison de Pipaix*, for the spiced version[48].

Breweries located in Flanders also offer beers that come close to *saisons*. In particular, the Kerkom Brewery has *Reuss*, a well-hopped blonde beer blended with lambic; the De Ranke Brewery (in Wevelgem) has *XX Bitter*, an example of a light beer that is still highly hopped; and Dolle Brouwers (in Esen) has *Oeral*. As curious as it might seem, certain beers from the Cantillon Brewery in Brussels also help us to understand the taste of the old *saisons* that were sour and aged in casks: the *Cantillon Gueuze* and, in particular, *Iris*, which is an all malt beer that is spontaneously fermented, brewed with amber-tinged malt (of the pale ale type), flavored with both fresh and aged hops, and benefiting from a generous dry hopping.

Other breweries offer more "modern" versions are completely interesting and of a high quality. This is the case with Brasserie des Géants, in Irchonwelz, with its remake of *Saison Voisin* and Ellezelloise (in Ellezelles), with the *Saison 2000*, and, even though it is described as a wit beer, the *Blanche des Saisis*. Other Wallonian breweries and a Flemish brewer as well offer beers called *saison*, but which, in my opinion, completely usurp this name by proposing products that are syrupy and fruity to the extreme, possibly tasting of caramel and having nothing to do with this family of beers.

Authentic *saisons*, along with traditional lambic beers, are certainly the most fascinating among the styles of old beers that still exist in Belgium. Unfortunately they are part of a family of beers that is endangered since they no longer appeal to the tastes of the consumers who have become used to sweet and simplified flavors; therefore we absolutely must support or revive them in their authentic version or else they shall become extinct.

ACKNOWLEDGMENTS

My warmest thanks go to the following brewers who, during interviews or via correspondence, permitted me to better define what *saisons* were like in the past and how they have evolved over time: Claude Allard, former microbiologist at Dupont Brewery in Tourpes; Marie-Noëlle Pourtois, brewer at Blaugies Brewery; Marc Rosier, former brewer at Dupont; Léon Voisin, former brewer at Voisin Brewery in Flobecq (which stopped production in 1989); Jean-Louis Dits, brewer at Brasserie à Vapeur (the Steam Brewery) in Pipaix; Pierre-Alex Carlier from Blaugies; and Olivier Dedeycker, brewer at Dupont. Thanks also to Phil Markowski for giving me this opportunity (and for making such exquisite beers!), to B.R. Royla and Daniel and Will Shelton for the translation of this text.

ENDNOTES

[1] In De la bière, sa composition chimique, sa fabrication, son emploi comme boisson, (Paris: Baillière, 1861), p. 327.

[2] "L'industrie de la bière", in Les merveilles de l'industrie, ou description des principales industries modernes (Paris: Furne, Jouvet et Cie, 1880), p. 328. P. 391. He briefly describes this type of beer: it was a brown beer, produced in Bavaria, called "*bière d'été*" (summer beer) or "*bière de garde*" (beer for keeping), brewed in December, January, or February, by decoction and with very bitter hops and spices. Fermentation took place with bottom fermenting yeast and was achieved slowly at temperatures close to 5-6 degrees Celsius, in barrels of pitched wood.

[3] G. Lacambre, Traité complet de la fabrication des bières et de la distillation des grains, (Brussels: Decq, 1851), p. 245. According to him, the month of March was considered to be very favorable for brewing beers for keeping: "the name *bières de Mars* (March beers) was given to a wide variety of beers for keeping that were generally brewed all through winter and at the beginning of spring."

[4] It is important not to confuse the *saisons* in general, sometimes called "*saisons d'été*" (summer *saisons*) with the *saison* de Liège (Liège *saison*) which was also brewed in winter but had the main difference of using a yeast that had very low attenuation. This beer was drunk after a minimum of three or four months of storage. It was sometimes kept for one to two years, according to G. Lacambre (op. cit., p. 377). One could thereby suppose that a wild and lactic fermentation developed, making the beer more attenuated and giving it a vinous character. It contained, aside from malted barley, a large proportion of wheat, malted spelt, and oats.

[5] G. Vanderstichele, La brasserie de fermentation haute, (Turnhout: Splichal, 1905), p. 280.

[6] Léo Moulin, Les liturgies de la table, (Antwerp: Fonds Mercator, 1988), pp. 103, 107.

[7] R. Pinon, "Recettes de bières de ménage en Wallonie", in Studium et Museum, Mélanges Edouard Remouchamps, (Liège: Editions du Musée de la Vie Wallonne, 1996), p. 104. Most farming villages had a communal brewery, that is to say belonging to the district of a local lord, or, later, to the commune, and able to be used by its inhabitants in return for a tax. According to the author, who cites A. Tichon, the farmers were in the habit of brewing there twice a year during the cold season.

[8] Op. cit., p 109.

[9] In Traité complet théorique et pratique de la fabrication de la bière et du malt, (Brussels: Decq, 1879), p. 412.

[10] In Essais sur la science pratique du brassage", (Brussels: Frentz et d'Henin, 1890), p. 307.

[11] Op. cit., p. 412.

[12] G. Lacambre, op. cit. (1851), p. 320.

[13] G. Vanderstichele, op.cit. (1879), p. 280.

[14] G. Lacambre, op. cit., p. 244.

[15] Ibid., pp. 413, 414.

[16] Op. cit., p. 342.

[17] Op. cit., p. 324.

[18] G. Vanderstichele, ibid., p. 288.

[19] G. M. Johnson, ibid., p. 339.

[20] G. Lacambre, ibid., p. 56.

[21] J. Cartuyvels and Ch. Stammer, ibid., p. 413; G. Vanderstichele, op. cit., p. 288.

[22] J. Cartuyvels et Ch. Stammer, ibid., p. 464.

[23] J. Cartuyvels and Ch. Stammer, ibid., p. 414; G. Lacambre, op. cit., p. 320.

24 For example, by G.-F. Crendal, Lettre sur la bière, (Valenciennes: Henry, 1734), (reprinted Lille: Les éditions du bibliophile, 1987), p. 20.

25 Since a similar method is described in the book of J.-B. Bauby, Guide pratique de fabrication de la bière, (Strasbourg: Fosset Frères, 1867).

26 In "La Chimie des fermentations", Brasserie, vol. 2, (Paris: Masson, 1942), p. 185.

27 In Livre de poche de l'apprêteur de bières, (Brussels: Laurent Frères, 1871), pp. 54-55.

28 Marc Van Laer, "Les Brettanomyces", Le Petit Journal du Brasseur, no. 1087 (Brussels: 16 July 1920), p. 621.

29 No. 996, 5 December, p. 1727.

30 Le Petit Journal du Brasseur no. 20 of 18 August 1899, p. 296.

31 Op. cit., p. 321.

32 R. Pinon, op. cit., p. 109.

33 G. Lacambre, op. cit., p. 244.

34 A. Laurent, Traité théorique et pratique de la clarification des bières, vins, eaux-de-vie, cognacs, liqueurs et vinaigres, (Brussels: Laurent Frères, 1872), p. 42; G. M. Johnson, op. cit., p. 378.

35 Op. cit., pp. 64-66.

36 Th. Flinz, Le progrès de la brasserie, (Brussels: Lebègue, 1878), pp. 102, 121.

37 A. Laurent, Livre de poche de l'apprêteur de bières, (Brussels), op. cit., pp. 48, 54-56.

38 Op. cit., p. 413.

39 A. Laurent, ibid., p. 65.

40 Ibid., p. 79.

41 (Brussels: Laurent Frères, 1875), pp. 75, 272, 309.

[42] See for instance Auguste Laurent, who dedicated an entire work to this question in 1873: La bière de l'avenir (The Beer of the Future), (Brussels: Laurent Frères). See also H. Codvelle, "Pour concurrencer les bières étrangères", Le Petit Journal du Brasseur, no. 1072, (Brussels, 2 April 1920), p. 284 s.

[43] R. Pinon, op. cit., p. 108.

[44] At the Dupont Brewery, the "leaven" has been cultivated since 1950. It is however, as indicated above, composed of several yeast strains, of which at least one was "wild" in order to conserve the complexity of their beers.

[45] R. Pinon, op. cit., p. 106, tells us that in some regions the *saison* was called " Surette " ("tart").

[46] In Livre de poche de l'apprêteur de bière, op. cit., p. 69.

[47] "L'évolution de la Fermentation Spontanée", Le Petit Journal du Brasseur, no. 2091, (Brussels, 3 May 1946), p. 318.

[48] The fermentation of this one however has been a little bit "simplified" since the 1990s by the use of one sole top fermenting yeast strain and cylindro-conical fermenters in place of open ones. Jean-Louis Dits, the brewer, has nonetheless kept the equipment to permit him to remake a *Saison* in the old way, in open fermentation tanks, permitting him to benefit from a supplemental wild insemination. He is ready to relaunch it if the demand emerges.

seven

The World of Saison

Ask ten Belgian brewers "What is a *saison?*" and you'll likely get ten different answers. Nearly all will give a response that is tauntingly vague. "It must be refreshing," some will say. "They must be low in alcohol," others will insist. Least specific, they might reveal, "It is a beer made for the season." These vague and varied descriptions will frustrate anyone foolish or stubborn enough to try to pin down these wildly complex, deceptively simple rustic ales originally made primarily on farms in the French-speaking southern half of Belgium. *Saisons* defy easy categorization and are sometimes rife with contradiction. Many are light in color, a few are dark, and some are in between. One or two are full-bodied and sweetish, most are extraordinarily dry and fruity. Those who like their beers neatly arranged in narrow categories find defining *saisons* frustrating, to say the least. To others, this elusive quality is precisely their allure; they represent endless possibilities within a loose structure. In short, with *saisons*, almost anything goes.

The history of *saison* is certainly interesting and it is fun to imagine what these rustic farm brews must have tasted like, but no one alive can know for certain. What matters is what is available in the modern world. Clearly *saisons* have evolved over time to become less rustic as improvements in brewing science, not to mention the invention of artificial refrigeration, transformed even the most rural breweries.

The historical purpose of farmhouse ales was to sustain and refresh laborers. If we classify modern farmhouse ales as either "refresher" or "sustainer" we can find commercial versions of Belgian *saison* that fit either category. A few modern versions of *saison* fall into the sustenance category, full-bodied sweetish versions such as *Saison Silly* from Brasserie Silly and *Saison Regal* from Brasserie DuBoq. Most modern versions fit the refresher bill quite well. Best known is the distinctive *Saison Vieille Provision* from Brasserie Dupont, considered by many to be the standard-bearer for the style.

Several *saisons* are made with spices, a throwback to earlier times. *Saison de Pipaix* from Brasserie à Vapeur, *Saison 1900* from Brasserie Lefebvre, and the lineup of seasonal *saisons* from Brasserie Fantome all contain varying degrees of spices. Recently developed versions are *Saison 2000* from Brasserie Ellezelloise, *Saison Voisin* from Brasserie des Géants (a remake of an old regional *saison*), and *Saison d'Epeautre* from Brasserie Blaugies, which uses a form of wheat called *epeautre* (spelt) in the grist. A few Flemish brews such as *Bink Blonde* from Brouwerij Kerkom (perhaps the oldest continuously operated farm brewery in Belgium) and *Martens Seizoens* have fruity, dry, hoppy accents that place them closer to *saison* than to any other recognized Belgian style. Adding to the puzzle are three products from a small brewery, Brasserie Baillieux in France, just over the border from Belgium. One is confusingly labeled *Saison Saint Medard—Bière de Garde de L'Avesnois*, another is *Saison Saint Medard—Bière de Noel*. A third product, *Cuvee des Jonquilles* (*jonquille* means daffodil, suggestive of a seasonal or spring brew), fits the classic *saison* profile with a dry, hoppy, fruity palate —yet it is the only product of the three that contains no reference to *saison*. It plainly has *Bière de Garde de L'Avesnois* written on the label.

GRISETTE

As the landscape of Hainaut province began to shift from an agricultural to a coal and stone mining region in the late 1800s, local brewers began to market a beer to the growing population of miners. As *saison* was considered the drink of farm workers, *grisette* was the brew of the miners. The origins of the name are sketchy (*gris* means gray in French). Grisette is commonly said to refer to young women who worked in factories and wore a distinctive gray frock as a uniform. As one story goes, these young women, *grisettes*, would hold trays of ale to refresh the workers as they exited the mines. The term has also been attributed to the color of the porphyritic stone mined in the area of northern Hainaut province.

At least one regional brewery, Brasserie Lefebvre, successfully marketed a beer directly to the miners under the name *Porph Ale*. The brand is no longer produced. According to Belgian beer enthusiast Joris Pattyn, no fewer than 30 brands of grisette existed in the heyday of the Belgian mining industry. Nowadays the miners are very few and only a single brewery markets the name grisette. Brasserie Friart, producers of the *St. Feuillien* brands, has three types of grisette: blond, witbier, and amber. This example of nostalgic marketing is similar to that employed by some French *bière de garde* breweries (namely Brasserie Castelain) who have seized a once familiar style name and used it as a pseudo brand name under which to market several "colors" of beer.

Oral accounts of those who remember the old grisettes say they were low-alcohol, light-bodied, *saison*-like golden ales of

no great distinction. Indeed the intention was to be dry and refreshing as is the case with *saison*. According to Leon Voisin, retired brewmaster of Brasserie Voisin, grisettes were relatively clean blond ales of 3 to 5% alcohol content that mimicked the refreshing character of *saison* (only hops were the source of "refreshing" character as opposed to lactic acid sourness of "old" *saison*). Annie Perrier-Robert and Charles Fontaine, authors of *Belgium by Beer, Beer by Belgium*, offer the following description of grisette: "The wort measures 6.5 to 7 °Belgian (16.3 to 17.5 °P, 1.065 to 1.070 SG); long boiling gives the beer its amber colour."

SUPER SAISONS

When a brewer becomes known for producing a *saison*, consumers have a tendency to think of that brewery's entire product line in a similar light. This appears to be the case with Brasserie Dupont, now famous for its distinctive *Saison Vieille Provision*, but not long ago better known for a strong golden ale called *Moinette*. The distinctive *Moinette* and the outstanding 9.5% strong ale *Avec Les Bons Voeux De La Brasserie* ("with the best wishes of the brewery," originally brewed as a New Year's gift to special clients) have been informally called "super *saisons*" by aficionados (as has *Dupont Brune* been called a "brown *saison*"). While present brewmaster Olivier Dedeycker insists that these are simply specialty ales, he has reluctantly used the term "super *saisons*" to categorize his distinctive strong ales.

As consumers have developed a preference for higher alcohol specialty beers, brewers have been happy to oblige their customers with increasingly stronger brews. Nearly all modern *saison* brewers acknowledge that at a typical 5 to 6% alcohol by volume, their present-day *saisons* are stronger than is considered traditional. In fact, some upstart *saison* brewers, notably Brasserie Fantome, seldom, if ever, produce a *saison* below 7% alcohol. The bestselling brand from Brasserie à Vapeur is not *Saison de Pipaix*, but the 9% *Vapeur Cochonne*, also dubbed a super *saison* by aficionados. It is inevitable that over time the bar is raised not only by Belgian but also North American brewers who often interpret classic styles with a "bigger is better" enthusiasm. These bigger, stronger versions add dimension and depth to the family of brews collectively known as *saison*.

So that's the landscape of *saison*. As with *bière de garde*, this overview sets the stage for a closer look at the style's characteristics both through generalized descriptions and through examination of the individual beers being produced in both Europe and America.

eight
Drinking Saison

*I*n this chapter will we focus on the flavors and other attributes of *saison*. We'll begin with "classic" *saison*, a deep golden to amber colored ale of conventional (4 to 6%) alcohol strength that exhibits the typical fruity, spicy aromatics associated with the style. Established "Old World" versions are the models for this classic version.

APPEARANCE

The typical color for *saison* is a deep golden to light orange hue in the range of 6 to 8 °SRM. There are lighter versions and those that approach a deep amber color (*Saison Silly* is the darkest at roughly 23 to 25 °SRM). A slight haze (most are unfiltered) is common and a rocky head is a trait in these brews, testament to their generally all-malt composition and higher-than-average carbonation levels.

AROMA

Saisons generally possess classic fruity, ale-like aromatics. Several versions have a distinctive spicy (notably pepper) yeast character as well as typical ale-like esters (apricot, bubble gum, banana) with a notable reduction in classic clove-like phenols typical of other Belgian specialty ales. Hop aroma can be very low to high with earthy, spicy varieties the most commonly used. Spices, assorted botanicals, and other unusual additives may be employed to give *saisons* distinguishing characteristics that are not normally derived using conventional beer ingredients. Potential sources of additional aromatic complexity are wild yeasts, lactic bacteria, and a cork closure to the bottle.

FLAVOR

A wide range of flavors exists in *saison*, most often of fruity/spicy description. These characteristics are often contributed by the yeast but can be enhanced by the addition of various herbs and spices. Hop bitterness is generally noticeable but not in the pale ale sense. Hop flavor and aroma can be described as low to medium in intensity. Flavor is typically dry and refreshing with fruit and spice flavors most dominant.

Lactic sourness may be present in more rustic examples and adds a dimension of historical accuracy. A brief mention of the *saison* style in a 1946 edition of the Belgian brewing publication *Le Petit Journal du Brasseur* likens *saison* to gueuze due to a characteristic lactic sourness found in many versions of *saison* at that time. It is impossible to say if this lactic character was intentional or if it resulted from less-than-rigorous cleaning and sanitation practices at these rural breweries. References indicate that old, sour beer, probably from the previous brewing season, was typically blended with new "top-fermented" beer in an effort to give the young beer more flavor. No doubt there was motivation to use up the old ale as little was wasted on the farm, but intentionally soured beers have a long history and a strong

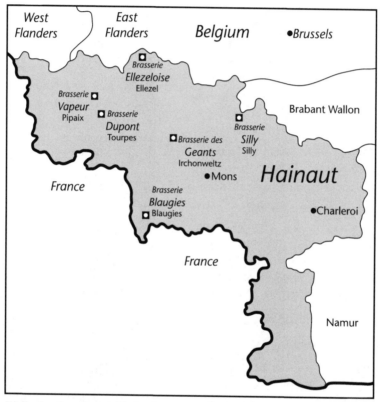

Wallonian Farmhouse Ale Producers
The Hainaut area of the Wallonian section of Belgium hosts modern-day producers of saison.

Review of Classic Saison Characteristics

- *Saisons* generally have a complex fruit and spice-driven aroma and notably lower phenol character than most Belgian ales. Such characteristics may be purely the result of yeast strain selection or may come from the use of spices or other botanicals, a throwback to older brewing techniques.

- Generally *saisons* are extraordinarily well attenuated and can be quite lean and dry in body and mouthfeel.

- *Saisons* are often hopped more aggressively than most Belgian ales. Emphasis is most often on hop aromatics and flavor rather than on hop bitterness.

- Color is usually pale in modern *saison*; an orange hue is considered the classic color.

- *Saisons* often possess a certain charm or rusticity, a hard-to-define earthiness or *terroir*, a French term generally applied to wines that refers to the net result of the conditions (soil, weather, microclimate) relating to where a crop is grown. Additional earthiness may result from a cork finish and/or possibly from yeast interaction during bottle-conditioning or extended aging.

following in this region. Modern *saisons*, notably the range of Fantome products and occasionally *Saison de Pipaix*, sometimes display a lactic sourness, especially when they have been aged in the bottle for a period of time.

BODY

Saisons are generally well attenuated with apparent final gravities in the range of 0.5 to 2.0 °P (1.002 to 1.008 SG). Even the full-bodied versions such as *Saison Silly* measure in the range of 1.5 to 2.0 °P (1.006 to 1.008 SG). The apparent degree of attenuation in Belgian *saisons* typically measures in the range of 85 to 95%, suggesting residual sugar levels well

Physical Parameters of a Sampling of Commercial Belgian Saisons

Product	Original Gravity (P)	Apparent Final Gravity meas.(P)	Alcohol By Volume	Apparent Degree of Attenuation	*Bitterness (IBUs)	*Color (SRM)	*Color (EBC)
Dupont Saison Vieille Provision	13.5	1.0	6.3	93%	32	5.5	11
Blaugies Saison D'Epeautre	12.0	0.5	5.8	96%	n/a	n/a	n/a
Ellezelloise Saison 2000	12.0	0.6	5.7	95%	n/a	n/a	n/a
Fantome Printemps	16.5	1.5	7.5	91%	n/a	n/a	n/a
*Geants Saison Voisin	12.0	1.3	5.4	89%	29	13.5	27
*Lefebrve Saison 2000	14.4	1.0	6.7	93%	n/a	7	14
Saison Regal	12.4	0.9	5.8	93%	20	16.5	33
Saison Silly	11.6	1.6	5.0	86%	15	23.5	47
Vapeur Saison de Pipaix	13.0	1.1	6.0	92%	n/a	n/a	n/a

Table 7. Comparison of original gravity, measured apparent final gravity, alcohol content, and apparent degree of attenuation of some commercially available Belgian *saisons.*

*Information provided by Derek Walsh, testing performed by De Proef Brouwerij.

below most non-adjunct brews. Many examples—*Saison d'Epeautre* from Brasserie Blaugies is probably the most dramatic—display a body and mouthfeel that seem fuller than the measured terminal gravity (0.5 °P, 1.002 SG in the case of *Saison d'Epeautre*). The latter example uses 33% *epeautre* (spelt) in the mash, as it has higher protein content than wheat and contributes the impression of a fuller mouthfeel and body as well as a dense long-lasting head of foam.

ALCOHOL CONTENT
Traditionally *saisons* fall into the range of 3 to 5% alcohol by volume. This follows logic that they are not to be made too strong as they are intended to refresh, not to inebriate. Present day consumers have come to expect specialty ales to contain higher alcohol content than everyday Pilsener beers, for example. Consequently, alcohol content of even the most traditional *saisons* has crept up over the years as upstart revivalist Belgian brews and new world interpretations of *saison* are typically found to be in the 6 to 9% alcohol by volume range.

MODERN PRODUCERS OF BELGIAN SAISON
As we have throughout this book, we'll begin our look at the specific beers produced in this style in Europe and then move on to examine the upstart American versions.

BRASSERIE BLAUGIES—BLAUGIES, BELGIUM
This tiny garage brewery (it literally occupies the family garage) is located in the traditional farming town of Blaugies, a stone's throw from the French border. The brewery was started in 1988 by a husband-and-wife schoolteacher team inspired by an ancient beer recipe they found in an old text-

book. The couple was helped by (now retired) Brasserie Dupont brewmaster Marc Rosier and brewmaster Emile Cavenaile of the defunct Brasserie Cavenaile, regarded as two of the finest brewers of the region. Now one of the couple's sons does the brewing (mom used to) and the other runs the adjacent restaurant. The brewery has a revivalist slant; it produces a *saison*-like beer fermented with fig juice called Darbyste, based on a local tradition of consuming fig juice that had mysteriously been previously fermented. The flagship product is *Saison d'Epeautre*, a particularly dry version of the Wallonian style brewed with a portion of *epeautre* (spelt), a traditional culinary grain in Belgium and France. The use of spelt in Blaugies *Saison d' Epeautre* recalls the farmhouse tradition of using a variety of raw grains (most likely whatever was available at the time) in the brewing of *saison*.

Warehouse at Brasserie Dupont.

Saison d'Epeautre
Specifications:
Original Gravity: 12.0 °P (1.048 SG)
Apparent Final Gravity: 0.5 °P (1.002 SG)
Alcohol By Volume: 6.0%
Apparent Degree of Attenuation: 95%
Malts: Belgian Pilsener 67%, raw, dehusked *epeautre* (spelt) 33%
Hops: Styrian Goldings
Yeast: Proprietary ale yeast
    (an extraordinarily attenuative strain)
Primary Fermentation Temperature: 77-80° F (25-27° C)
Garding (Storage) Period: 5 days at 41° F (5° C)
Tasting Notes: Dry wheaty notes with a fresh "sea air" aroma accompanied by cork and yeast notes. Extraordinarily dry and refreshing, a great old world version. The lower alcohol content, very high attenuation, and subtle hop character make Sasion d'Epeautre possibly the most historically accurate version on the market today.

Brasserie Dupont—Tourpes, Belgium

In the late 1980s importer Don Feinberg of Vanberg & DeWulf of Cooperstown, New York was looking for a new beer to add to his growing portfolio of specialty beers. At the urging of Michael Jackson he paid a visit to Brasserie Dupont and met with then-brewmaster Marc Rosier to see about importing *Saison Vieille Provision* into North America. Rosier was puzzled by the American's interest in their least popular product—why not *Moinette*, their bestseller? Feinberg stuck to his mission to make the *saison* widely available in the United States. That noble effort, along with the praise of Jackson and others, has made this example the clear benchmark of the style. Subsequently, *Saison Vieille Provision* has become the flagship brew of Brasserie Dupont, with good reason. It is a wonderfully complex brew that projects a vast range of intermingling flavors and aromas.

The present formulation of *Saison Vieille Provision* is said to date from the 1920s, and is actually brewed on an operating farm (they also make outstanding cheeses). Brasserie Dupont's brews possess an undeniably rustic character with a more aggressive hop character than other Belgian *saisons*. Fermentation esters and hop aromatics dominate the aroma and flavor of *Saison Vieille Provision*, which, the brewmaster insists, contains no spices. The brewery produces a couple of unique stronger ales, *Moinette* (16.5 °P, 1.066 SG) and *Avec Les Bon Voeux de la Brasserie Dupont* (18.5 °P, 1.074 SG) which some people like to call "super *saisons*." Current brewmaster Olivier Dedeycker dismisses this notion because these brews are "too alcoholic" to be *saisons*. *Saisons* are meant "to refresh the worker, they should not be too strong." The brewer admits with a sly smile that *Saison Vieille Provision*, at 6.5% alcohol by volume, is stronger than is classic for the style.

Saison Vieille Provision
Specifications:
Original Gravity: 13.5 °P (1.054 SG)
Alcohol By Volume: 6.5%
Apparent Degree of Attenuation: 93%
Malts: 100% Dingeman's Pilsener Malt
Hops: East Kent Goldings and Styrian Goldings
    (in two additions)

Yeast: House ale yeast
Primary Fermentation Temperature: 85-95° F (30-35° C)
Storage Period: 6-8 weeks in the bottle at 74-75° F (23-24° C)
Other Characteristics: Centrifuged and unpasteurized.

Tasting Notes: A wonderful aroma full of tropical fruits, fresh sea air, and earthy hops on a solid malt background; there is also a hint of cork and even "light-struck" character (in this case it is not unpleasant). Very well balanced with a fruity/spicy finish. World class.

Brasserie Fantome—Soy, Belgium
If any single brewery embodies the unbridled spirit of *saison* brewing, it would be Brasserie Fantome—eccentric, idiosyncratic, not to mention variable. Owner/brewer Dany Prignon is a free spirit, to put it mildly, and his personality is reflected in his line of products—whimsical and generally unpredictable. Brasserie Fantome opened in 1988 in the small country hamlet of Soy, in Luxembourg province southeast of Brussels. The

brewery produces a traditional *saison* called *Fantome*, but is probably best known for its four *Saison d'Erezée* (*Erezée* is the greater commune where Soy is located) brews that are made for the four seasons, *Hiver* (winter), *Printemps* (spring), *Ete* (summer) and *Autome* (fall). Each of these brews is made with a variety of "secret" ingredients (spices, herbs, fruit juices), vary (sometimes greatly) from year to year, and are meant to evoke the specific season. The brewery has made a *saison*-like brew called *Pissenlit*, flavored with dried dandelion flowers.

Saison d'Erezée Printemps
Specifications:
Original Gravity: 16.5 °P (1.066 SG)
Alcohol By Volume: 7%
Malts: Pilsener and Munich
Hops: Hallertauer
Yeast: Ale yeast
Primary Fermentation Temperature: 82° F (27.5° C)
Garding (Storage) Period: 6 days at 37° F (3° C)
Other Characteristics: Candy sugar is used
    (in unknown proportions).
Tasting Notes: Hoppy, sourish notes with grassy/lemony aromatics. Has a curious quinine-like bitterness as well as lemon rind and a mineral, chalky finish. Funky and refreshing in a classic *saison* sense.

Brasserie des Gèants—Irchonweltz, Belgium

The "Giant Brewery" opened in 2001 by Pierre and Vinciane Delcoigne in a refurbished medieval castle in the town of Irchonweltz, near Ath in the south of Belgium. The brewery is named after the Parade of Giants, which takes place in nearby Ath each year and features a larger-than-life effigy of Goliath, or *Gouyasse* in the local dialect. The brewery's principal product is *Gouyasse*, a 6% blonde ale that has quickly earned the brewery a reputation as a high-quality upstart producer of traditional Belgian ales. The young couple is well qualified for brewery work; Pierre is a graduate brewery engineer, and Vinciane a chemist. It doesn't hurt that they are passionate about beer and the art of brewing.

Brasserie des Gèants has revived a local beer, *Saison Voisin*, formerly brewed by Brasserie Voisin (which closed in 1989; Brasserie des Gèants now uses some of the old equipment) in nearby Flobecq. The current recipe (minus the use of wild yeast) is said to date back to 1895. Leon Voisin, retired brewmaster of the original version, has proclaimed the new *Saison Voisin* an accurate reproduction of the original.

Saison Voisin
Specifications:
Original Gravity: 12 °P (1.048 SG)
Alcohol By Volume: 5%
Apparent Degree of Attenuation: 90%
Malts: Belgian Pale, Munich, and Caramel
Hops: Kent Goldings from Belgium
Yeast: Proprietary ale yeast
Primary Fermentation Temperature: 77-82° F (25-28° C)
Garding (Storage) Period: 2 weeks at 35° F (2° C)
Other Characteristics: All-malt grist, no spices added.
Tasting Notes: A deep orange-amber color with a slight haze. Yeasty/hoppy aroma with notes of peaches, orange and earthy, grassy hops. Bitterness is noticeable, more assertive than most, but balanced by a rather firm, toasty maltiness.

Brasserie à Vapeur—Pipaix, Belgium

A working industrial museum of sorts, Brasserie à Vapeur is owned and operated by Jean-Louis Dits, a fulltime history teacher with a passion for beer, particularly the local specialty, *saison*. Dits purchased the brewery in 1986 and was mentored by Marc Rosier, at that time the acting brewmaster at Brasserie Dupont. Dits hosts a legendary "open brew" session on the last Saturday of every month, when he fires up the ancient steam turbine (it takes the previous day to get everything ready) and somehow manages to make the whole wheezing, shaking mass of antique machinery brew a batch of beer in just under eleven hours. The present brewery building dates back to 1890 and the recipe used for *Saison de Pipaix* allegedly dates back to 1785 (Dits has a "black book" that he found in the brewery that supposedly contains this recipe; farmhouse marketing at work?). The brewery produces only 450 U.S. barrels per year with *Saison de Pipaix* accounting for approximately 10% of that volume (despite Dits' original intention that this brew would be the flagship, only one batch is produced per year). *Vapeur Cochonne*, with its sexy label, accounts for 70% of total production, unfortunate proof that packaging is king even at one of the most traditionally minded breweries in the world.

Dits is fond of spices and uses them in most of his brews. He claims to have tutored Dany Prignon of Brasserie Fantome (and perhaps influenced his definition of *saison* as a spiced and flavored brew). Dits' daughter recently received a university degree in brewery engineering and is becoming increasingly involved in the brewery, helping to make improvements in the brewhouse to make the products more consistent.

Saison de Pipaix
Specifications:
Original Gravity: 13.0 °P (1.052 SG)
Alcohol By Volume: 6 %
Apparent Degree of Attenuation: 92%
Malts: 58% Pilsener, 40% Vienna,
    and 2% amber (30 °L, 60 °EBC)
Hops: Hallertauer, Kent Goldings, and Styrian Goldings
Yeast: Various local sources (does not brew often
    enough to maintain a house culture)
Primary Fermentation Temperature: 76° F (24° C)
    (lasts one week)
Storage Period: 4-6 weeks at 37° F (3° C)
Other Ingredients: A blend of spices including black pepper,
    sweet orange, curaçao orange, ginger, star anise, and lichen
    (Dits claims to still add it in spite of reports to the con-
    trary) added fifteen minutes before the end of the boil.
Other Characteristics: All-malt, unfiltered, and unpasteurized.
Tasting Notes: Decidedly rustic with woody, fruity, iron notes
on top of a malty, dryish sour backdrop. The flavor is peppery,
fruity, and dry; refreshing and pleasantly funky. A true farmhouse ale.

NEW WORLD SAISON PRODUCERS

Brewery Ommegang—Cooperstown, New York
Brewmaster Randy Thiel is a Wisconsin native, a degreed microbiologist, and a passionate scholar of Belgian ales. Thiel began
his brewing career in 1997 when he joined Brewery
Ommegang, founded by importer Don Feinberg, responsible

for bringing the revered Brasserie Dupont *Saison Vieille Provision* into the United States. Acknowledging *Saison Vieille Provision* as a classic example of the style, the folks at Ommegang decided that they wanted to put their own stamp on a brew inspired by Dupont's and other *saisons* they have tasted (the brew was formulated by original brewmaster Bert de Wit). The result was *Hennepin*, a complex and distinct *saison*-like brew (inspired by the lesser known *grisettes*) named after Father Louis Hennepin, a Belgian missionary who accompanied LaSalle in mapping and exploring the Midwestern United States.

Hennepin
Specifications:
Original Gravity: 16.8 °Plato (1.067 SG)
Alcohol By Volume: 7.7%
Apparent Degree of Attenuation: 87%
Malts: Pilsener and pale malts
Hops: Styrian Goldings (bittering), Czech Saaz (finish)

Yeast: Proprietary ale yeast

Primary Fermentation Temperature: 77° F (25° C)

Garding (Storage) Period: 2 weeks at 32° F (0° C)

Other Characteristics: Dextrose added to the brew kettle to boost fermentable sugar content; flavored with a blend of spices. Bottle conditioned.

Tasting Notes: A complex nose that is, appropriately, difficult to describe. Hot peppery spice, apples, bananas, dried leaves, and candied pears combine with a doughy vanilla malt backdrop. The flavor is spicy and refreshing. A distinct and reverent interpretation.

McKenzie Brewhouse—Chadds Ford, Pennsylvania

McKenzie Brewhouse was established in 2001 in a busy suburb within commuting distance of downtown Philadelphia. Brewmaster Scott Morrison has quickly developed a reputation for producing a wide range of seasonal brews, particularly Belgian-style interpretations. One of the most popular is *Farmhouse Saison,* now brewed several times yearly where the majority is bottled for sale at the brewpub. *Farmhouse Saison* is strongly influenced by Dupont's *Saison Vieille Provision,* one of Morrison's "all-time favorite beers."

McKenzie Farmhouse Saison

Specifications:

Original Gravity: 13.5 °P (1.054 SG)

Alcohol By Volume: 6.2%

Apparent Degree of Attenuation: 92%

Malts: 100% Dingeman's Pilsener

Hops: East Kent and Styrian Goldings

Yeast: Brasserie Dupont Culture

Primary Fermentation Temperature: 82° F (28° C)
to start with free-rise to 90° F (32° C)
Storage Period: 1 week at 50° F (10° C)
Other Characteristics: Bottle-conditioned for 6 weeks
at 70° F (21° C)
Tasting Notes: Classic Juicy Fruit gum aromatics, upfront hop character, vanilla malt, and spicy, peppery notes. Flavor is well balanced with a hint of hop bitterness and just a touch of sourness in the finish.

Pizza Port—Solana Beach, California

Brewmaster Tomme Arthur has developed a solid reputation for his pedal-to-the-medal, adventurous interpretations of Belgian ales. He brews in San Diego and has the decidedly New World approach of aging his more exotic old world inspired ales in barrels that literally sit on the sand not far from the Pacific Ocean. With a nod toward the Fantome Brewery he makes numerous *saison*-style brews, each with an array of spices and exotic flavorings. He brews a different *saison* for different seasons (not that such a thing exists in San Diego). Appropriately, they don't have labels like "winter" and "summer" but names such as *SPF 8, SPF 15,* and *SPF 45* since they are brewed in a city said to have one of the most ideal year-round climates in the world.

Pizza Port SPF 8
Specifications:
Original Gravity: 21.2 °P (1.085 SG)
Alcohol By Volume: 9.6%
Apparent Degree of Attenuation: 91%

Malts: Pilsener, Caramel Wheat, Melanodin, Special B,
and Carafa II

Hops: Amarillo and Tettnanger

Yeast: Two strains of ale yeast—one for flavor (Dupont) and
one for attenuation

Primary Fermentation Temperature: 74° F (22° C)

Storage Period: Unavailable

Other Characteristics: Inspired by Fantome *Black Ghost.*
Flavored with caramelized raisins deglazed with port wine,
and spiced with fresh rosemary and orange peel.

Tasting Notes: Deep brown color with a vigorous head of
foam. The aroma is very complex, if a little subdued compared
to the flavor, which is full of toffee, chocolate, fruit, spice, and
a woodsy/piney note (the rosemary?) on top of a substantial
malt backbone. Unique and inspired.

nine
Brewing Saison

The history and culture of a style hold great interest for beer drinkers, but for anyone who has ever participated in the brewing of a beer, true intimacy with a style cannot be achieved until you know the details of how it is brewed.

In this chapter, we begin by reviewing what we know about the production of *saison* in Belgium before moving on to discuss the techniques and materials favored in North America.

BELGIAN BREWING PRACTICES

Let us begin our look at the brewing of *saison* with a detailed review of what we know from practicing Belgian makers of this style.

Water

The water in most Wallonian farmhouse breweries comes from wells and, as is the case in the surrounding region, is moderately high in temporary hardness (bicarbonate). Minerals such as carbonate and sulfates have the net effect of emphasizing hop character and perceived dryness in elevated quantities. A water profile such as that shown in Table 8 would yield enough residual alkalinity to warrant pH buffering with an acidifying agent. Most brewers in this region opt to add food-grade lactic acid in order to counteract the natural alkalinity of the native water.

Typical Saison Brewing Water

Brewery #1	
pH	7.2
*Bicarbonate	350
Calcium	52
Chloride	20
Magnesium	17
Sodium	35
Sulfates	107
Total Hardness	454

Table 8. Water analysis from a classic *saison* brewery (quantities shown are in mg/l).

*Indicates a calculated figure.

Malt

Saisons have generally been brewed using the lightest colored malts, which today yield straw to deep golden colored brews in the range of 6 to 8 °SRM (depending on brewhouse conditions). A light amber/orange color in the range of 10 to 14 °SRM is considered to be the classic color. Many modern *saison* brewers choose to add a small portion of higher kilned malts, typically Vienna or Munich, to a base of Pilsener or pale ale malts in an effort to replicate this color. Others (Dupont, for example) prefer a lighter color and use 100% Pilsener malt in their grist formulation.

Unconventional Brewing Grains

Various non-traditional grains were apparently used in the brewing of *saison* in the past. Grains besides barley and wheat (oats, rye, etc.) were grown on farms that also brewed *saisons*. There is every reason to believe that, for practical reasons, a variety of different grains (raw or malted) would make their way into a farmhouse mash. Additionally, for several decades of the nineteenth century, unmalted brewing grains were taxed at a lower rate than malt, providing an extra incentive for their use. Examples of this legacy appear in a few revivalist *saison*-like brews such as the *Joseph* and *Sara* brews from Brasserie Silenrieux (the brewery opened in 1992). The former uses spelt and the latter buckwheat in the grist. Another example exported to the United States is *Saison d'Epeautre* from Brasserie Blaugies (which opened in 1987). Epeautre, or spelt (*Triticum spelta*), one of the world's oldest cultivated grains, is a distant relative of wheat (*Triticum aestivum*) that traces its origins (as does beer) back to ancient Mesopotamia. It remains a popular culinary grain in France, Belgium, Italy, and Germany.

Mashing

Most of the *saison* breweries interviewed for this book use a classic step infusion mash, with emphasis on maximizing production of fermentable sugars. A typical mash program used by a traditional *saison* brewer starts with a protein rest at 113° F (45° C) for thirty minutes, then it is heated to 131° F (55° C) with a rest for fifteen minutes. The mash temperature is then raised to 144° F (62° C) for a thirty-minute saccharification rest, followed by a fifteen-minute dextrine rest at 154° F (68° C), and finally mash off at 165° F (74° C).

Note: Brasserie Dupont uses a different approach, favoring a "rising temperature" infusion mash. Dupont starts with an initial temperature of 113° F (45° C) and continuously heats the mash (while constantly stirring) by approximately 0.5° F (0.25° C) per minute over the course of 108 minutes (1:48) until the mash temperature reaches 162° F (72° C). The intention is to maximize fermentable sugar production in order to get the characteristic attenuation (when an appropriate yeast strain is used) and low terminal gravity of 1.0 to 1.5 °P (1.004 to 1.006 SG).

Hops

Hop bitterness is typically restrained and is more evident in the flavor and aroma of Belgian *saison* (as is the case with Brasserie des Géants *Saison Voisin* and especially in Dupont's *Saison Vieille Provision*). Some of the fruitiness and earthiness of *saison* is contributed directly from the hops, which work in concert with yeast aromatics in the better examples. The most common varieties are Kent Goldings (from Belgium and sometimes from the UK) and Styrian Goldings. Other Continental varieties such as Brewers Gold and Hallertauer have reportedly been used but appear less popular.

Spices

Spices are used by many, but by no means all, contemporary Belgian *saison* brewers (Brasserie Dupont, Ellezeloise, and Brasserie des Gèants are three who claim to use no spices at all in their *saisons*). The use of spices in brewing is a throwback to the days before the widespread use of hops. Two modern *saison* producers in Belgium celebrate their use of spices, various botanicals, and other unconventional additives; they are *Saison de Pipaix* from Brasserie à Vapeur, and the Fantome brewery.

Yeast

Belgian brewers are well aware of the possibilities of using yeast as a major contributor to beer flavor. All modern *saison* brewers appreciate this fact, albeit to varying degrees. There are those who use a relatively expressive yeast but choose to complement (or bowl over) the yeast character with spices. A few, most notably Brasserie Dupont, use a highly expressive yeast strain to its full potential to do all the talking, providing plenty of spice character without actually adding spices.

Some commercial Belgian *saisons* have been known to develop sourness and occasionally "barnyard" characteristics, presumably from *Brettanomyces* or other wild yeasts. These char-

USE OF DIFFERENT YEAST STRAINS IN THE BREWERY

Many small-scale brewers are convinced that using different yeasts strains in the same brewery is a really bad idea. The concern is probably more intense when considering Belgian-type yeast strains valued for their unique fermentation byproducts. The premise is that different strains will no doubt infiltrate one another, making them "impure" and subsequently wreaking havoc in the brewery. This information likely trickled down from larger industrial brewers who rely on common manifold systems to transfer beer and wort throughout their breweries. In this type of arrangement it is easy to understand how the use of multiple yeast strains could be a problem.

With disciplined use of standard cleaning and sanitizing procedures hundreds of small breweries consistently make good, stable beer while unseen swarms of airborne wild yeasts and bacteria inhabit their breweries. If we can effectively combat spoilage from these organisms there is no reason why we can't successfully use different yeast strains in our breweries.

acteristics tend to assert themselves over the course of months, even years, of storage in the bottle. Whether these characteristics are desired or not (explanations may vary depending on the drinker's reaction) is not clear, but such characteristics have been associated with particular breweries, notably Fantome and Vapeur. In any case some lactic sourness in *saison* is still considered appropriate by some Belgian beer aficionados, whether intentional or not.

Bottle Conditioning

Saisons are traditionally bottle-conditioned, and that fact resonates with today's Belgian *saison* brewers who universally choose to bottle-condition their products. Typically, the beer is given fourteen to twenty-one days (Dupont allows forty-two to fifty-six days) to condition in a temperature-controlled environment (in the range of 72 to 75° F) and then, after testing for physical and sensory parameters, terminal gravity, carbonation, flavor, and aroma, the product is released for sale.

PRACTICAL FORMULATION GUIDELINES

Having looked at the Belgian materials and techniques, let us now move to consideration of how best to brew this style in America. The following guidelines offer parameters from which to formulate your own version of *saison*. Bearing in mind the range of interpretations on the market today, these guidelines are general but nonetheless a reference point to create your unique example.

Typical Physical Parameters

Original Gravity: 11 to 14 °P (1.044 to 1.056)

Apparent Final Gravity: 0.5 to 2.5 °P (1.002 to 1.010)

Apparent Degree of Attenuation: 80 to 95%

Bitterness: 18 to 32 IBU

Color: 3 to 18 °SRM (6 to 36 °EBC)

Water

Recall that brewing water in the Hainaut region of Belgium tends to be high in temporary (bicarbonate) hardness. (See Table 8.)

Considering that a dry, refreshing character is a classic attribute of traditional Belgian *saison*, a brewer may wish to increase the sulfate content of the brewing water. This step is best accomplished by adding calcium sulfate. Additions of calcium sulfate will have the extra benefit of driving mash pH downward if your brewing water is naturally alkaline (as is typical of Wallonian breweries). Calcium sulfate additions (when combined with heating the water) may provide adequate buffering by rendering the bicarbonate insoluble in water, forcing it to precipitate out as a solid. This depends on the inherent alkalinity of the water as well as the amount of calcium sulfate added to the base water. Each water source is different and finding the right mix requires a certain amount of trial and error.

Increased amounts of sulfate ion will have the net effect of intensifying perceived dryness and hop character. Sulfate levels above 100 ppm will most certainly enhance perceived dryness in beer flavor. For replicating a classic Belgian *saison* it is not recommended that the sulfate content be greater than 300 ppm, as at these levels beer flavor may become too bitter and "minerally" than is typical for classic *saison*.

Alternative methods of countering alkalinity are an addition of food-grade lactic acid or a small percentage (typically 1 to 2% of total grist for a moderate degree of alkalinity) of acidulated malt in order to buffer the natural alkalinity of the water and to lower the pH of the mash to the desired range of 5.4 to 5.6. Once again finding the right amounts to add requires trial and error. Before making any additions it is advisable to obtain a recent analysis to gain an accurate understanding of your water's mineral composition.

Refer to Table 9 for guidelines in adding calcium sulfate to your brewing water.

Mineral Addition Guidelines

Rate of Addition (CaSO₄)		Mineral Contribution, ppm	
grams/gal.	oz./bbl	Calcium (Ca)	Sulfate (SO4)
0.5	0.6	30	74
1	1.1	60	148
1.5	1.6	90	222
2	2.2	120	296

Table 9. Amounts of individual calcium and sulfate ions contributed by the addition of calcium sulfate (gypsum) to brewing water.

Grist Formulation

There are, of course, countless possible grist formulations that could be used in brewing *saison*. The simplest approach (favored by Brasserie Dupont) is a mash of 100% Pilsener malt. On the other end of the spectrum, a brewer may draw inspiration from *saison*'s history of being brewed on farms from a combination of malted barley and whatever grains were available at the time. That thought conjures up limitless possibilities of using either raw or malted wheat, spelt, oats, or rye grains typically found on the European table. The possibilities are limited only by the brewer's imagination.

In practice, most brewers stick with malted barley and its own infinite permutations and combinations. The general approach taken by most Belgian brewers is to obtain an orange to amber hue from the use of modest amounts of Vienna or Munich malts on top of a base of Pilsener or pale malts. The quantities listed below are merely suggestions; for insights into how a few commercial *saisons* are formulated refer to the section at the end of this chapter entitled Modern Producers of Belgian *Saison*.

Options:

    Use of up to 30% Vienna malt (by weight)
    Use of up to 40% malted or unmalted spelt
    Use of up to 40% unmalted or malted wheat (by weight)
    Use of up to 2% color malt (by weight)
    Use of up to 10% sucrose (by extract) for higher gravity interpretations

Mashing

Choose a mash temperature program that emphasizes production of fermentable sugars. *Saisons* typically have apparent terminal gravities in the range of 0.5 to 2.0 °Plato (1.002 to 1.008) assuming the use of a highly attenuative yeast culture. Either a single temperature infusion mash or step infusion is normally used. If using a single temperature infusion it is recommended that the saccharification temperature be on the lower end, in the range of 143 to 147° F (62 to 64° C) in order to maximize fermentable sugars.

Hop Usage Considerations

The following guidelines are based on information obtained from commercial Belgian brewers and from my own experiences. Once again, they are suggestions and represent a basis from which to make your own unique formulation. For further suggestions see the suggested recipes at the end of this chapter.

Hopping (Bitterness)

The hops used by Belgian *saison* brewers are generally Continental varieties grown in the Poperinge area of Belgium. Belgian-grown Kent Goldings are a popular choice as are Styrian Goldings, followed by Czech Saaz and German Hallertauer.

Bittering Charge

A target range is 18 to 32 IBUs, depending on such factors as original gravity, grist composition, and yeast strain selection. For leaner, dry examples choose a bitterness level near the low end of the spectrum. Belgian brewers generally like the hop bitterness in the distance; *saisons* are an exception. Still the bitterness in *saison* is seldom as forceful as in typical pale ale. The choice is ultimately the brewer's preference.

Example

In the following example we are targeting 24 IBUs using East Kent Goldings hops (5.6% alpha acid) with a known alpha acid extraction efficiency of 30%.

Target bitterness of 24 IBUs (mg/l) with a 30% extraction rate requires that we add 24 mg /0.3 or 80 mg/l alpha acid to the brew kettle.

At 5.6% alpha acid (East Kent Goldings hops, 2003 crop) this means that we need to add 80 mg/0.056 alpha or 1,429 mg (1.43 grams) East Kent Goldings hops per liter of wort.

1 U.S. barrel = 117 liters (5 U.S. gallons = 18.9 liters)

This results in a hop bittering addition of East Kent Goldings hops (5.6% alpha acids) of 1.43 grams x 117 liters, which is equal to 167.3 grams/U.S. barrel or 5.8 oz. East Kent Goldings hops/U.S. barrel.

0.36 lbs./U.S. barrel or 26.7 grams/5 U.S. gallons of East Kent Goldings hops (5.6% alpha acid) to obtain 24 IBUs

Flavor Hops

Hops are generally present in the aroma of *saison* ranging from "detectable" to assertive. Hop character helps define the refreshment aspect of a classic *saison*. Examples that are spiced tend to follow the rule to keep hop intensity low in order to display the spice character more readily. In the best examples, hops combine with fermentation esters or spices, or both, to create the unique, complex aroma profile of a textbook *saison*.

A brewer may approach hop additions in a similar manner as they might with pale ale in terms of the timing of the additions—a flavor hop addition at fifteen to twenty minutes before the end of the boil, and a finish hop addition during the last few minutes of the boil. The latter addition is generally on the order of two to three times larger than the flavor addition (in the case of Brasserie Dupont, the hoppiest Belgian example, there is no flavor addition but simply a bittering addition and a sizable charge added during the last minute of the boil).

The following suggestions are intended to result in a moderate hop intensity using classic hop varieties.

Note: The suggested quantities listed in the following sections are for a saison without added spices. If adding spices these suggested hop additions should be reduced on the order of one-half to two-thirds in order to better display spice character.

Late hop addition (15 to 20 minutes before end of boil).

Using East Kent Goldings or noble hop varieties.

Based on addition to wort boil 15 to 20 minutes before the end of the boil.

For a moderate to high level of aroma and flavor, a late hop rate of 0.20 to 0.25 pounds (3.2 to 4.0 ounces) per U.S. barrel might be considered appropriate. This translates to approximately 0.50 to 0.60 ounces (15 to 18 grams) per 5 U.S. gallons. Certainly, a brewer may add more or less hops than suggested and naturally other varieties may be substituted, preferably earthy, spicy varieties such as Styrian Goldings, Saaz, or Hallertauer.

Note: At this hopping rate using East Kent Goldings (at 5.6% alpha acid), the amount of late hop bitterness contributed (at fifteen to twenty minutes boiling time) would add between 6 to 8 IBU to the final brew. Be sure to include that amount in your overall bitterness calculations.

Aroma Hops
The following suggested amount will result in a moderate to high level of hop aroma in the brew. Styrian Goldings are used in this example but the brewer is free to use any noble aroma hop either exclusively or in a blend. A suggested blend, for

additional depth of character, might be 50% Styrian Goldings, 30% East Kent Goldings, and 20% Saaz as a starting point.

Aroma hop addition (last one to two minutes before end of boil) of 0.4 to 0.5 pounds (6 to 8 ounces) per U.S. barrel or 1 to 1.25 ounces per 5 U.S. gallons.

Note: Using Styrian Goldings (3.4% alpha acid for the 2003 crop) the bitterness contributed can be practically taken as negligible.

Dry Hopping (optional)

0.25 to 1.0 oz.   0.1 to 0.2 lbs.

Dry hopping is optional but not practiced by any of the Belgian producers that we visited (Brasserie Dupont discontinued the practice some time ago in favor of a larger last-minute boil addition). Suggested rate of addition ranges from 0.1 to 0.2 pounds (1.6 to 3.2 ounces) per U.S. barrel or 0.25 to 0.50 ounces per 5 U.S. gallons.

Some Suggested Spice Quantities

SPICE	*Ounces per barrel	*Grams per 5 gallons
Coriander	1.5 - 2.5	7.0 – 12
Cumin	0.1 – 0.25	0.5 – 1.2
Curaçao/bitter orange	1.5 - 3.0	7.0 - 14
Ginger	0.1 - 0.25	0.5 – 1.2
Grains of paradise	0.1 - 0.20	0.5 - 1.0
Star anise	0.1 - 0.20	0.5 - 1.0
Sweet orange	1.0 – 2.0	5.0 – 10.0

Table 10. Suggested range of optional spice additions for brewing *saison*.

Note: Quantities suggested range from "barely detectable" to "noticeable" in terms of aroma and flavor. Quantities indicated are of very finely ground dried spices.

Spices

The use of spices in brewing *saison* is optional, not a requirement as many brewers seem to believe. While several commercial Belgian *saison* brewers use spices, just as many do not. Too often, a "more is better" approach is taken (Belgian brewers are just as guilty of this) and the beer flavor becomes smothered by spice character. When using spices, less is often more. Used sparingly, especially in a blend, individual spices are not easily identifiable. Instead, they can add unique complexity in the form of aromatics and flavors that leave the drinker guessing, wondering, and ideally, wanting for more.

Besides quantity, an important variable to consider is when the spices are added to the brew. The addition of spices can be thought of in much the same way as adding hops to a brew. Spices may be boiled for a period of time to extract flavors (including bitterness, in the case of curaçao orange) at the expense of diminished aromatics. If a "cleaner" spice aromatic is desired, spices added at the end of the boil (or post fermentation, in a "dry spiced" approach) will yield a fresher individual character (boiling tends to mute the spice character, but seems to assimilate it more permanently into the brew). Most commonly they are added to the boil in the last ten to twenty minutes. As with hop additions, the timing and quantities of spice additions require experimentation and are ultimately the choice of the individual brewer. One point to keep in mind is that more can always be added if the desired intensity is not achieved with earlier additions. Once a brew is over-spiced the only course of action the brewer can take is to blend in unspiced beer to dilute the flavor to an acceptable level, a luxury most of us do not have.

Table 10 shows suggested quantities of some of the more commonly used spices in *saison* brewing. Suggested amounts range from "detectable" to "noticeable" in overall presence. Ideally, one shouldn't be able to detect them individually. Quantities cited refer to spices that have been very finely ground in order to release essential oils and to expose the maximum surface area. Ideally, the spices should be dried but reasonably fresh (fresh ginger or orange peel for example would contain an unknown amount of water weight) and ground just prior to adding to the brew so that the essential oils are at their most potent. These quantities are merely guidelines; adding more or less of any spice is always the choice of the individual brewer.

Boiling Time

Although extraordinarily long kettle boils were common in the past, today's commercial *saison* brewers employ a typical one-and-a-half to two-hour boil. Motivation for long boil times in the past were to darken the wort color and provide stability, as was a commonly held belief of that time.

Fermentation

The use of a highly attenuative aromatic yeast strain is a very important contributor of character in *saison*. The obvious choice is the Brasserie Dupont culture, not solely because of the familiarity of their *Saison Vieille Provision*, but because of the complexity of flavors and aromatics that this unique strain produces as well as its ability to be super-attenuative (when given the time). Other Belgian yeast strains are available that offer plenty of fruity complexity, especially when used at elevated fermentation temperatures in the 75 to 80° F (24 to 27° C) range.

THE BRASSERIE DUPONT STRAIN—
A YEAST AMONG YEASTS

One of the most distinctive and complex yeasts in the brewing world is that used by Brasserie Dupont for their specialty products, notably the flagship *Saison Vieille Provision*. Under the right conditions it produces a vast array of aromas and flavors— white pepper, mango, passion fruit, clove, bubble gum (Juicy Fruit, anyone?), and general tropical fruit notes. This yeast differs from many other Belgian ale strains in that its production of classic clove-like phenols and isoamyl acetate (banana ester) are notably less intense (on a sensory level, anyway) than is typical of most Belgian yeast strains. It is eccentric yeast, and there is a price to pay for such intrinsic complexity. It can exhibit sluggish behavior at temperatures below 75° F, and ferment rapidly and relatively cleanly at blood-warm temperatures (upper 80s to 95° F). Other times it can suddenly and inexplicably shut down as if hitting a wall, slowing to a frustrating

A DIFFERENT APPROACH

Learning more about winemaking was an eye-opener to different approaches to fermenting and processing alcoholic beverages. In some cases, brewing farmhouse-style ales (*saison*) is closer to winemaking than it is to lager brewing. For example, learning that red wines typically ferment in the range of 80 to 95° F helped me to realize that exceeding the limits of fermentation temperature might not result in Armageddon after all. Indeed, pushing the envelope beyond what I previously thought was a wise and prudent brewing procedure that often resulted in a more authentic beer.

snail's pace of fermentation. At this point (in spite of higher temperatures and with plenty of yeast visibly in suspension) it can work excruciatingly slowly, sometimes taking weeks to finish fermentation if you let it (I think it is worth the wait).

The sluggish end fermentation may be due to an inherent inability to easily ferment maltose, maltotriose, and other polysaccharides. In normal fermentation activity the enzymes necessary to break down complex fermentable sugars into glucose units are produced internally in the yeast cell. The ability of yeast to readily produce these (hydrolyzing) enzymes varies from strain to strain and is, in part, influenced by the growth

FERMENTATION TEMPERATURES—HOW HIGH WILL YOU GO?

Most North American brewers are well acquainted with lager fermentation techniques and the emphasis on low temperature fermentation for clean flavor, which is the correct approach for lager brewing. What about the upper temperature limits of fermentation? We've read in British brewing texts that these should be in the range of 68 to 70° F. This may be comfortable for us and for most yeast, but is it ideal for all strains? Most of us have witnessed certain (British) yeasts strains that refuse to work at temperatures below 65° F. We may have also used yeasts that produce "clean" ales while fermenting at temperatures in the 70° F range. So isn't it possible that some strains may still work cleanly or even produce desirable esters at temperatures in excess of 75° or even 85° F? What's good for one strain of yeast may not be for another and what matters most is the taste of the finished product. The only way to find out is to step out of our comfort zones and experiment. All it takes is an open mind (and a bit of nerve) to make some interesting discoveries.

media. It should be noted that this tendency for sluggish end-fermentation activity is more noticeable in first propagations. In this case the yeast strain may be capable of fermenting only monosaccharides (the simple sugars that are the first consumed at the onset of fermentation and generally comprise about 15% of the fermentable sugars in a typical all-malt wort). In an extreme example, another strain (either contained within a mixed culture or one added by a brewer) must then take over to ferment the more complex sugars.

Besides being extraordinarily expressive in terms of aroma and flavor production, the Dupont yeast is highly attenuative and is said (by some) to be a multi-strain culture comprised of at least four different organisms, all of the *Saccharomyces* genus (at least one strain is thought to have originally been a wild yeast), according to Olivier Dedeycker, brewmaster at Brasserie Dupont. Chris White of White Labs,

Fermentation at 30° C equals 86° F—a level unknown in most types of brewing.

whose laboratory has observed more than one distinct culture, supports that suggestion. However, after isolating these cultures they have identified one strain that seems to be dominant in exhibiting the characteristic Dupont aromatics. Les Perkins, quality control manager at Wyeast Labs, states that in examining the dregs from bottles of *Saison Vieille Provision* they have found only single cell morphology indicative of a single

IT TAKES A VILLAGE—MULTI-CULTURE FERMENTATIONS

The idea that their brew could be fermented with more than one strain or culture of yeast is frightening to some brewers. The notion seems to suggest impurity or contamination. This concept may be scary to someone of the mindset of single strain purity in German brewing and alien to those accustomed to the quick fermentation/aging cycles of classic British ales. These multi-culture fermentations take more time, often on the order of weeks or months, depending on factors such as temperature and cell counts. An extreme example is the lambic family of brews, which can take years, by the traditional method, to complete the succession of fermentations needed for full flavor development.

More subtle examples are traditional *saisons* and witbiers, which traditionally can acquire lactic sourness over time, and some Trappist styles such as Orval. In the latter, major flavor changes occur over weeks and months of storage as strains of the *Brettanomyces* genus slowly break down some of the complex sugars that the *Saccharomyces* yeasts have left behind. This is another example where Belgian brewing philosophy is different than what most of us are used to and an example of where the Belgian brewing approach resembles (red) winemaking, where multi-culture fermentation (i.e. the malolactic fermentation that follows the main ethanol-producing fermentation) is standard operating procedure.

yeast culture. (The jury is still out on this issue. Both White Labs and Wyeast labs market a single cell version of this yeast strain that in the author's experience will produce comparable complexity to results obtained from manually culturing the yeast from the dregs of a bottle of *Saison Vieille Provision*. Perhaps Dedeycker's "four strain" claim is genuine but it would seem to pose a formidable challenge to maintain a consistent balance of these four strains of culture and wild yeast in both a lab and practical brewery environment.)

Perkins has a theory that the Dupont strain may have originally been a red wine yeast that over time adapted itself to a brewery environment. Perkins and several co-workers have observed (independently of each other) that under controlled growth conditions in the lab (using a malt sugar-based growth medium) the Dupont strain exhibits a strikingly similar aromatic profile to many red wine cultures (as compared with lager and ales cultures) which he cites as "low in phenols and rich in fruity overtones." Common physical characteristics between the Dupont culture and a typical red wine yeast include the ability (or preference) to work at unusually high temperatures (typically 77 to 90° F or 25 to 32° C) without excessive fusel alcohol production as well as the capacity to be super-attenuative (which indicates an exceptional ability to produce hydrolyzing enzymes to break down complex sugars, albeit very slowly). Under practical fermentation conditions the Dupont yeast's sometimes sluggish performance is commonly seen with red wine cultures, which are known to have a higher free amino nitrogen (FAN) requirement than typical ale and lager yeasts. Winemakers routinely add DAP (diammonium phosphate) to their wine musts in order to specifically boost FAN levels.

Whether or not the Dupont strain is a descendent of red wine yeast is not only an interesting point to ponder, it may provide some insight into sidestepping an unusually long primary fermentation. Adding an increased amount (perhaps double the recommended rate) of yeast nutrient will provide additional FAN and other important micronutrients so that this yeast has adequate nutrition to complete the fermentation relatively quickly (this effect may not be noticeable on a practical level, however). An experimental brewer might want to add DAP (per manufacturer's instructions) to the fermentation in order to test the increased FAN requirement theory of the Dupont strain. While it

IF YOU LOVE IT, LET IT GO

"Fermentation" does not necessarily mean only the visible kraüsen stage of obvious activity. In some examples it can be a very slow, barely detectable action that, if given the time, will produce noticeable, sometimes profound flavor changes to the brew. In order to allow these slow fermentations to take place the brew must be allowed to rest at a relatively warm temperature (65 to 75° F) for a period of one to several weeks, depending on temperature, cell counts, pH, and available sugars. Some of the distinct yeast cultures used by Belgian brewers continue to work after the visible main fermentation is completed (they work very slowly, but are working nonetheless). These unusual yeasts will continue fermenting, slowly breaking down polysaccharides if they are allowed to do so, which means given the time (two to six weeks, typically) and temperature (65 to 75° F, 18 to 24° C), they will reward you with flavor.

(Note: It should be pointed out that if a beer is to be warm-aged for a period of a few weeks, it should be racked off the sedimented yeast to avoid autolysis).

is unclear (in the author's experience) whether or not additional yeast nutrient has a definite positive effect in reducing fermentation time using the Dupont culture, it is reasonable to assume that adding it would not have a negative effect (other than the modest cost incurred). Some brewers have reported that "overpitching" (perhaps at a rate of one-and-a-half to two times more than normal) and aerating aggressively can help reduce the time needed to complete primary fermentation. This approach will theoretically preserve micronutrients (including FAN) by reducing the amount of cell growth needed to reach a typical saturation point of 50 to 60 million cells per milliliter. The fact is that this

TERMINAL GRAVITY—HOW LOW CAN YOU GO?

Some styles of Belgian beer have apparent terminal gravities that a brewer accustomed to English and German styles might find alarmingly low. The use of adjuncts, particularly in higher alcohol brews, as well as the occasional use of highly attenuative (sometimes multistrain) yeast cultures, results in low apparent final gravities, often in the range of 1.0 to 1.5 °P (1.004 to 1.006 SG) and sometimes lower. Some brewers are in the habit of crash-cooling a brew to inhibit further fermentation because they have been trained that a brew is done fermenting when it reaches a designated gravity rather than when all the fermentable sugars are consumed by the yeast. In the case of some Belgian ales, including traditional *saison*, the latter part of the fermentation can be sluggish as fastidious highly attenuative yeasts (or sometimes wild yeast or bacteria) slowly break down higher-order sugars (dextrins) into fermentable units. The production of lambic styles, where apparent final gravities are often very low (in the range of 1.0 °P or lower), is an extreme example of this phenomenon.

yeast appears to need time and the proper conditions (warmth, heavy aeration, and extra micronutrients) to work to full flavor potential. A brewer seeking the maximum character from this unique yeast will be rewarded by showing patience and avoiding reflexively "crash cooling" the brew, allowing the yeast to continue to work, however slowly, for up to a few weeks following the initial vigorous fermentation (it is suggested that the sedimented yeast be separated from the beer to avoid yeast autolysis). If a primary or secondary fermentation vessel cannot be tied up for an extended period, a "warm aging" period may be observed during keg or bottle conditioning of the brew. Regardless of where it takes place, it is suggested that an extended warm aging period of three to eight weeks be observed in order to obtain the maximum character from this distinctive yeast.

Primary fermentation using Dupont's yeast is an exercise in the abnormal and will test your willingness to think and act Belgian. It appears to go into near hibernation at temperatures below 70° F and seems to thrive at temperatures in the 85 to 95° F range—territory where few brewers dare to tread.

At Brasserie Dupont, primary fermentation proceeds at the shocking 85 to 95° F (30 to 35° C) and lasts for five to seven days. The reasons for the higher than usual temperatures are largely practical—the brewery lacks primary fermentation capacity and needs to ferment the brew as quickly as possible. The emphasis at Dupont is to get the initial active fermentation done within one week. This factor, rather than being seen as essential for flavor development (the yeast delivers plenty of character at 75 to 80° F, but the fermentation takes much longer—see note on page 77) appears to be the reason for the unusually high fermentation temperature. There is a curious parallel between Brasserie Dupont's approach to fermentation and a typical (red) winemaker's; the priority is to get the fermentation done as opposed to going after a particular ester profile. In fact, many red winemakers ferment in the range of 90 to 95° F and attemperate only to avoid killing the yeast.

Following one week in the primary fermenter the brew is transferred to a cool room for secondary fermentation at 65 to 70° F (18 to 21° C) when the gravity is in the range of (1.5 to 2.0 °P). After ten to fourteen days in the secondary fermenter the gravity slowly drops (the apparent final gravity is in the range of 1.0 to 1.2 °P or 1.004 to 1.005 SG) and the bulk of the yeast settles out. Following the secondary fermentation, the brew is centrifuged, dosed with priming sugar and fresh yeast, and then bottled. The bottles are stored in a temperature controlled "warm room" at 74 to 75° F (23 to 24° C) and conditioned in the bottle for a period of six to eight weeks before being released for sale. Curiously, the bottles are stored on their sides during

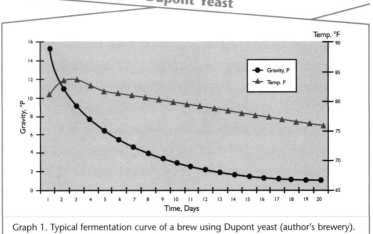

Fermentation Chart - Dupont Yeast

Graph 1. Typical fermentation curve of a brew using Dupont yeast (author's brewery).

the conditioning period. The brewer states that this keeps the corks wet, contributes cork character, and increases the surface area contact between the yeast and the conditioning beer (notice how bottles of *Saison Vieille Provision* have a film of sediment running down the length of the bottle).

The brewery feels that this extended warm aging is necessary to develop the signature character of *Saison Vieille Provision* (incidentally, brewmaster Dedeycker feels the beer tastes best at about six months of age) and will not release it sooner in spite of the cost of longer-term storage. Brasserie Blaugies, brewers of *Saison d'Epeautre*, bottle-conditions its products in a manner similar to Dupont.

Graph 1 shows an actual fermentation curve (author's brewery on a first propagation) that displays the characteristic rapid start followed by a progressively sluggish finish to the fermentation. The fermentation took a full twenty-one days to reach a terminal gravity of 1.2 °P (1.006 SG).

*A note on the upper limit of the fermentation temperature range cited. It is not essential to ferment this yeast upwards of 80° F in order to get complex character from the yeast. At temperatures in the 75 to 80° F range there is plenty of complexity contributed by this yeast. In fact, it seems that there are more desirable "tropical fruit" notes produced in this range while the higher end (85 to 90° F) seems to emphasize phenolics and higher alcohols. No doubt the fermentation will proceed quicker at the high end of this temperature range and it is used at Brasserie Dupont for largely practical reasons, as the brewery lacks primary fermentation capacity. At Dupont they choose to do their extended warm aging in the bottle (six weeks) as opposed to a secondary in-tank aging period. It is recommended that the brew be transferred shortly after the most visibly active phase of the fermentation is completed to avoid extended contact with sedimented yeast and trub.

Primary Fermentation

A highly attenuative aromatic yeast strain is an important contributor of character in *saison*. The obvious choice is the Brasserie Dupont culture, not solely because of the familiarity of *Saison Vieille Provision*, but because of the complexity of flavors and

Recommended Ale Yeasts for Brewing Saison

WHITE LABS	Suggested Fermentation Temperature	Degree of Attenuation	Comments
WLP565 Belgian Saison 1	80-95° F (27-35° C)	73-80%	Extremely fruity yeast. Very slow working at end. Highly attenuative.
WLP550 Belgian Ale	75-80° F (24-27° C)	72-78%	Very versatile, general purpose Belgian ale yeast. Spicy and fruity
WLP400 Belgian Wit	72-80° F (22-27° C)	65-70%	Classic Belgian yeast, ferments spicy and becomes somewhat tart over time.
WLP570 Belgian Golden Ale	72-80° F (22-27° C)	70-75%	Produces spicy, fruity (pear) esters. Vigorous fermenter.

WYEAST LABS	Suggested Fermentation Temperature	Degree of Attenuation	Comments
3724 Belgian Saison	80-95° F (27-35° C)	75-79%	Extremely fruity yeast. Very slow working at end. Highly attenuative.
3522 Belgian Ardennes	75-80° F (24-27° C)	72-76%	Very versatile, general purpose Belgian ale yeast. Spicy and fruity
3463 Forbidden Fruit	72-80° F (22-27° C)	75-79%	Classic Belgian yeast, ferments spicy and becomes somewhat tart over time.
3864 Canadian/Belgian	72-80° F (22-27° C)	75-79%	Produces spicy, fruity (pear) esters. Vigorous fermenter.

Table 11. Readily available yeast cultures from two of the major North American suppliers and their characteristics.

aromatics that this strain produces and its ability to be super-attenuative. Other Belgian yeast strains are available that offer plenty of fruity complexity, especially when used at elevated fermentation temperatures in the 75 to 80° F (24 to 27° C) range. When using either White Labs WLP565 or Wyeast 3724, refer to the essay on the Brasserie Dupont strain. When using other yeast strains, it is recommended that the upper fermentation temperature limits of that particular strain be observed to contribute maximum ester formation. Refer to Table 11 that lists suggested fermentation temperature limits. Naturally, brewers are encouraged to push the envelope beyond the "safe" limits posted in this table, which may lead to some interesting discoveries.

Secondary Fermentation
As previously discussed relative to the Brasserie Dupont strain, if a yeast is showing slow but steady activity following signs of vigorous fermentation, it is recommended that the brewer be patient and permit the yeast to reach absolute terminal gravity. In extreme cases this point may take a week or two to reach. During this phase it is recommended that the beer be racked free of sedimented yeast to avoid yeast autolysis. An unusually high degree of apparent attenuation is a distinct trait of a classic *saison* and this defining characteristic may take more time to realize. Patience is the key.

BOTTLE CONDITIONING
Aficionados and brewers alike accept that a bottle-conditioned brew possesses more character and complexity than the equivalent brew served on draft. The reason is continued interaction between the beer and the yeast over time. For that reason, bottle-conditioning is highly recommended when

packaging *saison*. Carbonation levels are generally quite higher in traditional *saisons* than in most other styles of beer and ale. On that note, extra care should be taken to be certain that the yeast has had ample time to complete the fermentation (see section on Secondary Fermentation). Accounts of super-foamy *saisons* (including commercial Belgian, domestic commercial, and homebrewed examples) are common, a testament to the tenacity of some of these yeast strains.

SAMPLE RECIPES

Saison - classic version

Malt Type	Color (ASBC)	Grist % by Weight
Pilsener	1.6	90.0%
Wheat Malt	3.5	10.0%

Bittering Hops: 20-25 IBUs
Suggested Variety: East Kent Goldings

Late Hop Addition (last 15-20 min. of boil)
2.5 oz./U.S. bbl (12 grams/5 gal.)
Suggested Variety: East Kent or Styrian Goldings

Finish Hop Addition (last 2 min. of boil)
7.0 oz/U.S. bbl (1.1 ozs/5 gal.)
Suggested Variety: East Kent Goldings,
Styrian Goldings and Saaz (in a blend)

Options:
1. Caramel Malt - add up to 2.5% for color and residual sweetness.
2. Sugar - add up to 5% for dryness
3. Unmalted Wheat - add up to 5%

Fermentation: Ale strain at 75-90° F
Expressive yeast such as White Labs WLP565
or Wyeast Labs 3724 recommended.

Secondary Storage: 4-6 weeks at 65-75° F
(note: Secondary storage may be conducted in bottles
or kegs during conditioning)

Original Gravity: 13 ° P (1.052 SG)

Comments
This recipe is based on a classic version that emphasizes hop character and distinct spicy/fruity yeast and fermentation byproducts.

Saison - spiced version

Malt Type	Color (ASBC)
Pilsener	1.6
Munich	14
Wheat Malt	4.5

Bittering Hops: 16-20 IBUs
Suggested Variety: Hallertauer (or any low-alpha variety)

Spice Addition (last 20 min. of boil)

Curaçao orange	1.5 oz./U.S. bbl	(7 grams/5 gal.)
Ginger	5 grams/U.S. bbl	(0.8 grams/5 gal.)
Star anise	2.5 grams/U.S. bbl	(0.5 grams/5 gal.)
Grains of Paradise	3 grams/U.S. bbl	(0.5 grams/5 gal.)

(note: Suggested quantities are for a "subtle" effect)

Options:
1. Caramel Malt - add up to 2.5% for color and residual sweetness.
2. Sugar - add up to 5% for dryness.
3. Unmalted Wheat - add up to 5%.
4. Spices - other than those listed may be added in any qty.
5. Hops - Finish or aroma hops may be added if desired
   (less than 3 oz./bbl or 14 grams/5 gal.)

Fermentation: Ale strain at 72-78° F
Yeast producing typical "Belgian" character suggested;
White Labs WLP550 or Wyeast 3522 are good choices.

Secondary Storage: 2-3 weeks at 60-70° F

Original Gravity: 13 °P (1.052 SG)

Comments:
Hop character is subtle to allow spice character to emerge. Spice quantities are low and in a blend so as to contribute a unique but not easily identifiable character to the brew.

Grisette

Malt Type	Color (ASBC)	Grist % by Weight
Pilsener	1.8	75.0%
Wheat Malt	2.5	25.0%

Bittering Hops: 16-18 IBUs
Suggested Variety: Hallertauer

Late Hop Addition (last 15-20 min. of boil)
3.5 oz./U.S. bbl (16 grams/5 gal.)
Suggested Variety: Styrian Goldings

Finish Hop Addition (last 2 min. of boil)
2.5 oz/U.S. bbl (12 grams/5 gal.)
Suggested Variety: East Kent Goldings

Options:
1) Unmalted Wheat - add up to 5%
2) Sugar - add up to 5% for dryness

Fermentation: Ale strain at 70-74° F
A workhorse Belgian strain such as White Labs WLP550
or Wyeast 3522 will yield good results.

Secondary Storage: 2-3 weeks at 65-70° F

Original Gravity: 11 °P (1.044 SG)

Comments:
This recipe is intended to produce a light, refreshing, lightly-
hopped golden ale with classic Belgian yeast character.

"Super" Saison

Malt Type	Color (ASBC)	Grist % by Weight
Pilsener	1.8	85.0%
Munich	14	7.5%
Wheat Malt	4.5	5.0%

White Sugar (contributes 1.5 °P or 8.5% by extract)

Bittering Hops: 20-24 IBUs
Suggested Variety: Hallertauer Tradition

Finish Hop Addition (last 2 min. of boil)
8.0 oz/U.S. bbl (1.3 oz./5 gal.)
Suggested Variety: East Kent Goldings

Options:
1) Caramel Malt - add up to 2% for color and residual sweetness.
2) Spices - Used as desired by the brewer

Fermentation: Ale strain at 75-90° F
Expressive yeast such as White Labs WLP565
or Wyeast Labs 3724 recommended.

Secondary Storage: 4-6 weeks at 65-75° F
(Note: Suggested warm storage period will increase
attenuation and perceived dryness).

Original Gravity: 17.5 °P (1.070 SG)
16° P (1.064 SG) from Malt
1.5° P (1.006 SG) from White Sugar

Comments:
A strong *saison* with an assertive hop aroma and flavor. An option
is to add spices; if recommended yeast strain is used it will add
plenty of spice character.

Ingredient Sources

FRENCH MALT

The largest specialty malt supplier in France is Malteries Franco-Belges, a division of the huge Soufflet group. Franco-Belges malts are available in the United States and the use of these malts provides a level of authenticity, with signature husky, spicy flavor characteristics.

Franco-Belges malts are available in the eastern United States through North Country Malt Supply of Rouses Point, New York, www.northcountry.com or 888-368-5571. In the West and Midwest, Franco-Belges malts are available from Mid-America Brewing Supply, www.midamericabrewing.com or 507-934-4975.

BELGIAN MALT

The most common specialty maltster is Dingeman's, a division of Cargill Malt. It is available nationwide through Brewer's Wholesale Supply, www.brewerswholesale.com or 800-816-8542. Based in Rhode Island, Brewers Wholesale Supply has satellite warehouses in Colorado, Nevada, and Florida for distribution throughout the United States.

Also available through Brewer's Wholesale Supply are the specialty grains of Malteries de Chateau or Castle Maltings, a small, start-up Belgian maltster dedicated to production of high quality specialty malts.

SPELT (EPEAUTRE)

Malted spelt is available by custom order from Weyermann Specialty Malt Company (they offer a chocolate spelt and are willing to custom malt "light" spelt in small quantities). There are minimum quantities and the price is at a premium. Contact Judy at Crosby & Baker of Westport, Massachusetts at 800-999-2440 for details.

Raw spelt is available in small quantities at many specialty foods stores and in bulk from Purity Foods of Okemos, Michigan. Check their Web site at www.purityfoods.com or contact them at 517-351-9231 for pricing and further information.

FRENCH HOPS

Strisselspalt hops are available in the United States through Hop Union of Yakima, Washington. Their Web site at www.hopunion.com has good general information on hops and their lineage. For available varieties call 800-952-4873.

Strisselspalt hops are also available in the United States through S.S. Steiner, Inc. based in New York City, www.hop-steiner.com or 212-838-8900.

SUGAR

A tantalizing variety of partially refined sugars, widely used for brewing in centuries past, are available from www.suarindia.com.

SPICES

L.D. Carlson Company of Kent, Ohio is a supplier of some of the more exotic spices and botanicals used in specialty brewing, including curaçao orange peel, grains of paradise seeds (aka Guinea grains and melegueta pepper), as well as a range of hard-to-find flavorings such as heather tips, wormwood, and elder-flowers. A complete catalog is available at www.ldcarlson.com or call 800-321-0315 for further information.

High-quality coriander well suited for brewing may be found at Indian groceries and mail-order spice sources.

A wide variety of spices are available from Pendery's Inc. of Dallas, Texas. See their Web site at www.penderys.com or call 800-533-1870.

Another source is Penzey's Spices of Brookfield, Wisconsin. They may be reached at www.penzeys.com or 800-741-7787. A second branch of the same family runs a chain of stores called The Spice House, www.thespicehouse.com. Both are high quality with a wide selection of spices.

YEAST

A wide range of yeast strains, including those referenced in this book, are available through the following suppliers:

White Labs, Inc. of San Diego, California, www.white-labs.com or 888-5YEAST5 (888-593-2785).

Wyeast Labs of Mount Hood, Oregon, www.wyeast.com or 541-354-1335.

References

BIBLIOGRAPHY

Daniels, Ray. *Designing Great Beers*. Boulder, CO: Brewers Publications, 1996.

De Clerck, Jean. *A Textbook of Brewing. Vol. 1*. London: Chapman & Hall, 1957.

DeLange, A.J. "Deconstructing Residual Alkalinity and Mash pH." *The New Brewer*, July/August 2003.

Evans, R.E. *The Beers and Brewing Systems of Northern France*. Birmingham, England: Institute of Technical Brewing, Midland Counties Section, 1905 (223–238).

Figuier, L. "L'industrie de la Brasserie," Les Merveilles de L'industrie: 1880.

Jackson, Michael. *Beer Companion*. Philadelphia, PA: Running Press, 1992.

Jackson, Michael. *Great Beers of Belgium*. Philadelphia, PA: Running Press, 1998.

Jackson, Michael. *New World Guide to Beer*. Philadelphia, PA: Running Press, 1988.

Mosher, Randy. *Radical Brewing*. Boulder, CO: Brewers Publications, 2004.

Noonan, Gregory J. *Brewing Lager Beers*. Boulder, CO: Brewers Publications, 1986.

Perrier-Robert, Annie and Charles Fontaine. *Belgium by Beer, Beer by Belgium*. Luxembourg: Schortgen, Esch, 1996.

Rajotte, Pierre. *Belgian Ales*. Boulder, CO: Brewers Publications, 1992.

Walsh, Derek. *Bier Typen Gids* ("Guide to Beer Types"). Utrecht, Netherlands: Kosmos Z&K, 2002.

Woods, John and Keith Rigley. *The Beers of Wallonia*. Wiscombe, England: The Artisan Press, 1996.

Woods, John and Keith Rigley. *The Beers of France*. Wiscombe, England: The Artisan Press, 1998

PERSONAL CORRESPONDENCE

The following individuals provided information used in the Bière de Garde chapters via personal correspondence.

Baker, Tom (Heavyweight Brewing); De Baets, Yvan; Dhaussy, Alain (Brasserie La Choulette); Dupont, Sylvie (Brasserie Grain d'Orge); Ebel, Jim (Two Brothers Brewing); Feinberg, Don; Giard, Jean-Jacques (Brasserie Duyck); Henry, Ben (Brasserie Henry); Mosher, Randy; Ricour, Pierre (Brasserie St. Sylvestre); Ricour, Serge (Brasserie St. Sylvestre); Royla, BR;

Shelton, Daniel; Thiel, Randy (Brewery Ommegang); Theillier, Michel (Brasserie Theillier).

The following individuals provided information used in the Saison chapters via personal correspondence.

Arthur, Tomme (Pizza Port Solana Beach); Debaets, Yvan; Dedeycker, Olivier (Brasserie Dupont); Delcoigne, Pierre (Brasserie des Gèants); Dits, Jean-Louis (Brasserie à Vapeur); Feinberg, Don; Morrison, Scott (McKenzie Brewhouse); Mosher, Randy; Royla, BR; Shelton, Daniel; Stinchfield, Matt; Thiel, Randy (Brewery Ommegang); Voisin, Leon (Brasserie Voisin—retired); Walsh, Derek.

Index

Page numbers in **boldface** refer to illustrations and/or captions.